Praise for In

MW00620416

St. Thomas More isn

for our times. Louis Karlin and David Oakley illuminate More's brave witness of conscience and help us think about our own loyalty to truth.

R. R. Reno | Editor of *First Things*

This short but immensely rewarding biography of Thomas More is especially welcome today. Laws and public opinion throughout the western world acutely challenge the consciences of Christians who stand with Truth in the face of power. Karlin and Oakley brilliantly bring More's example of fidelity to life for us. They also show beautifully how More's was not a somber or curmudgeonly witness, and even martyrdom, but rather that he exhibited the serenity and joy that all disciples of the Lord should show, even under the most trying conditions. The authors provide us ample reason to judge that Thomas More was indeed a "man for all seasons."

Gerard V. Bradley | Professor of Law at
the University of Notre Dame and
co-Editor of *The American Journal of Jurisprudence*

Louis Karlin and David Oakley have given us a scholarly yet short and highly readable treatment of how Thomas More himself understood the stance he took and decisions he made in the drama that culminated in his resignation from high office, arrest, trial, and execution. The authors reveal to us the mind of an extraordinarily gifted individual who was both a man of his time and someone who possessed the strength of character to do what almost no one else in his time and place—or any time and place—would do, namely, endure martyrdom rather than say what he believed to be false. If the secularist Robert Bolt in *A Man for All Seasons* gave us "More the existentialist," and Hilary Mantel, pushing a different agenda, gave us in *Wolf Hall* "More the hypocrite," Karlin and Oakley give us the historical More—explaining from More's own perspective why he refused to take the Oath of Supremacy demanded by King Henry VIII and why he insisted on remaining silent about his reasons for refusing.

> **Robert P. George** | McCormick Professor of Jurisprudence at Princeton University and Visiting Professor of Law at Harvard University

Karlin and Oakley have written the finest reflection on Thomas More that I've read in many years. Brief, absorbing and rich in essentials, the text is a great first encounter with More's witness— from his thinking on conscience, heresy and the law, to his experience of legal persecution and martyrdom. An exceptional portrait of an exceptional man and his convictions.

> **The Most Rev. Charles J. Chaput, O.F.M. Cap.** | Archbishop of Philadelphia

A true Catholic statesman must know how to integrate an unyielding commitment to his faith and a savvy ability to compromise on what is negotiable in order to get things done. This fine new volume shows Thomas More not only to be a true Catholic statesman. It also shows why he was rightly named their patron saint. The portrait of More that is drawn here can serve as a lesson for those who aspire to this vocation about what they must do first to form their consciences well.

> **Fr. Joseph W. Koterski, S.J.** | Professor of Philosophy at Fordham University

Inside the Mind of

THOMAS MORE

The Witness of His Writings

Louis W. Karlin and David R. Oakley

 Scepter

Published by Scepter Publishers, Inc.
info@scepterpublishers.org
www.scepterpublishers.org
800-322-8773
New York

Cover and text design by Rose Design

Library of Congress Cataloging-in-Publication Data

Names: Karlin, Louis W., author. | Oakley, David R.
Title: Inside the mind of Thomas More : the witness of his writings / Louis
    W. Karlin and David R. Oakley.
Description: New York : Scepter Publishers, 2017. | Includes bibliographical
    references.
Identifiers: LCCN 2017057373 (print) | LCCN 2018002020 (ebook) | ISBN
    9781594173196 (ebook) | ISBN 9781594173134 (pbk. : alk. paper)
Subjects: LCSH: More, Thomas, Saint, 1478-1535.
Classification: LCC B785.M84 (ebook) | LCC B785.M84 K28 2017 (print) | DDC
    282.092—dc23
LC record available at https://lccn.loc.gov/2017057373

ISBN: 9781594173134 (pbk.)
ISBN: 9781594173196 (ebook)

Printed in the United States of America

CONTENTS

INTRODUCTION

---·◦◦·---

O N MAY 19, 1935, Pius XI canonized Thomas More, and since then lawyers around the world have adopted More as their patron. And, on October 31, 2000, John Paul II, in response to thousands of requests from around the world, proclaimed him patron of statesmen, politicians, and lawyers:[1] "The life and martyrdom of Saint Thomas More have been the source of a message which spans the centuries and which speaks to people everywhere of the inalienable dignity of the human conscience. . . . Precisely because of the witness which he bore, even at the price of his life, to the primacy of truth over

---

1. Over 40,000 leaders from ninety-five countries attended the ceremonies in Rome in October 2000.

power, Saint Thomas More is venerated as an imperishable example of moral integrity."[2]

Is the Church correct in these pronouncements? Should he be patron of statesmen, politicians, and lawyers? Most people, after watching the film version of Robert Bolt's *A Man for All Seasons*, answer in the affirmative: More is a hero of conscience because he would not bend to the will of the king when it entailed denying the truth. That is an adequate answer; it captures his greatest achievement. At the cost of his life, he chose the truth rather than placating power and enjoying its perquisites. But only a complete knowledge of the circumstances surrounding that decision drives home his greatness. In this essay, we explore the challenges faced by More and propose answers to why we do well to honor him.

---

2. John Paul II, Apostolic Letter Issued Motu Proprio *Proclaiming Saint Thomas More Patron of Statesmen and Politicians* (October 31, 2000), 1. *http://w2.vatican.va/content/john-paul-ii/en/motu _proprio/documents/hf_jp-ii_motu-proprio_20001031_thomas -more.html.*

Today, as in all days, many have experienced penalties for not bending to the prevailing state orthodoxies. For them, More is an inspiration, a source of strength. His life rightfully inspires devotion and imitation. Given his principled resistance to state authority, we are not surprised that he should be the target of some of the most popular works in contemporary Anglo-American culture and entertainment. *Wolf Hall*,[3] a recent, highly-acclaimed historical novel by Hilary Mantel, and a television series, and a Broadway play based on the book, set out to overturn the traditional—historically accurate—portrait of More as a cheerful, witty martyr for conscience and to recast him as a religious bigot and an aloof sadist. The creators of these works do not misunderstand More. Rather, they realize what he stands for—for truth greater than the self—and they reject it. Nevertheless,

---

3. For a comparative analysis of *Wolf Hall* and *A Man for All Seasons*, see Karlin, "What Bolt Got Right and Mantel Got Wrong," *Thomas More: Why Patron of Statesmen?*, ed. Travis Curtright (Lanham: Lexington Books, 2015), 155.

the enlightened makers of contemporary culture cannot square their fictions with the facts about More's last years. In terms of political philosophy and jurisprudence, More's writings and lived statesmanship yield deep insights into the nature of personal liberty and illuminate the necessary limitations on the state's authority to bind individual consciences and determine or define religious orthodoxy. On the personal level, More remains an expert guide to the sometimes conflicting demands of conscience and civil obedience. He sets an example of courage, prudence and, above all, faithfulness and integrity. For those of faith, he is the fitting intercessor for divine aid to illumine the mind and strengthen the will, to make right judgments and stay the course of righteousness, despite the cost. Without regard to faith, More's sacrifice affirms us all as persons of conscience.

CHAPTER 1

More's Understanding
of Conscience

MORE DIED FOR CONSCIENCE. He refused to accept that Henry VIII's marriage to Anne Boleyn was legitimate and that the king in Parliament had the authority to compel a citizen to affirm the state's pronouncement. For that he resigned, was arrested, convicted of misprision of treason, and sentenced to life in prison. While incarcerated, he refused to acknowledge that Henry VIII was Supreme Head of the Church in England. For that he was convicted of high treason and executed. Meanwhile, with rare exception, the English bishops and statesmen capitulated. The contrast is simple and obvious. The more we learn about his final years, the more we appreciate his compelling example of individual adherence to the truth. But, first, however, we need to appreciate the nature of conscience for More, its proper formation, and the scope of its demands. There is a risk of substituting the current prevailing view of conscience for More's and, perhaps, of undercutting the magnitude of his sacrifice.

More's understanding of conscience is one with the Catholic Church's perennial teaching. To be clear, it is not simply an exercise of personal autonomy. For More and the Catholic tradition, man's nobility does *not* reside in the mere assertion of the self over and against the demands of the community or the state. To be sure, conscience has a significant, irreplaceable subjective component; but it also has an equally important objective component. "Moral conscience, present at the heart of the person, enjoins him at the appropriate moment to do good and avoid evil. . . . It bears witness to the authority of truth in reference to the supreme Good to which the human person is drawn, and it welcomes the commandments. When he listens to his conscience, the prudent man can hear God speaking."[1] Virtue implies the power to ascertain the truths of morality and faith, apply them to concrete situations, and adhere to those judgments despite the cost. Here is the objective component: this judgment aims to be in conformity with what is *truly* just and good according to natural reason and the law of God. An upright conscience, then, is informed by education and by the Word of God. There is a truth that one is obliged to seek out and to discern in all its demands; More's adherence to conscience is incoherent without a claim to truth.[2] "He believed in a created order

1. United States Catholic Conference, Inc., *Catechism of the Catholic Church* (Vatican City: Libreria Editrice Vaticana, 1994), no. 1777.

2. In this regard, Robert Bolt's play is, strictly speaking, historically inaccurate insofar as More (in the play) bases his opposition to the Oath of Succession solely on conscience's subjective component, with seeming indifference to objective truth: "What matters is not that it's true, but that I believe it; or no, not that I *believe* but that *I* believe" (emphasis in original). Bolt, *A Man for All Seasons: A Play in Two Acts* (New York: Vintage Books, 1990), 91.

which human beings could come to know and which included an objective law of nature written in the human heart, one that anyone can know by reason. . . . Conscience, then, provides the metaphysical foundation and the ultimate binding force of law, arising from the very structure of one's being and not merely as the result of threatened punishment."[3]

At the same time, the exercise of conscience is subjective because only the individual can judge for himself. Nobody is infallible; the judgment of conscience can err. Nevertheless, one is obliged to obey it. As the Church has always taught, "[a] human being must always obey the certain judgment of his conscience. If he were deliberately to act against it, he would condemn himself. Yet it can happen that moral conscience remains in ignorance and makes erroneous judgments about acts to be performed or already committed."[4]

---

3. Gerard Wegemer, *Thomas More on Statesmanship* (Washington, D.C.: Catholic University of America Press, 1996), 73.

4. *Catechism of the Catholic Church*, no. 1790.

Of course, one might be culpable of failing to inform his conscience, culpable of voluntary or semi-voluntary ignorance. Even then, however, one is not relieved of the responsibility of following the judgment of conscience. For More, as for the Church, conscience is founded upon a radical sense of freedom and corresponding responsibility: a person must seek the truth and do what he believes is right in light of the truth.

In the case of More, the question of adherence to conscience was tried in the crucible of the controversies concerning the vexed question of the unity of the Catholic Church. As he (but few of his countrymen) saw it, the Crown and Parliament were requiring him to affirm a falsehood, namely, that the Church in England could claim autonomy over Christian consciences, independent of the rest of Christendom and the pope in Rome. We should distinguish several stages in the personal and historical drama that ensued: resignation, arrest, and execution. In all these periods, More acquitted himself with a heroic adherence to the principle of the indivisibility of the Catholic Church. What distinguishes More's heroism was that it was not rash or single-minded, but characterized by prudence and exercised with integrity, that is, with due regard to other obligations—to his family, his own life, the realm and, even, the king—until adherence to the supreme Good made conciliation impossible.

CHAPTER 2

The King's Great Matter and More's Resignation

HISTORICAL AND LEGAL BACKGROUND

More resigned the chancellorship, the highest office in the realm, on May 16, 1532. That was the day after the Convocation of Clergy accepted the Submission of the Clergy, whereby the bishops surrendered their right to govern the English Church independently of the king. Thus, the Submission of the Clergy allowed the king to review and veto all legislation by clergy in convocation and to review all canon laws and prevent execution or enforcement of any canons in England. It established the king as *de facto* supreme legislator and judge of the Church in England. This arrogation of power served to shut down one of the most storied legal careers in the history of law and politics, and occasioned one of history's greatest examples of courage.

Called to the bar in 1501, More was considered one of the brightest lights of his generation, as evidenced by the invitation to give a prestigious series of annual lectures that same year. (More spoke on St. Augustine's *City of God* from a historical and philosophical, not theological, point of view.) From 1507 to 1518, he filled leadership positions at Lincoln's Inn, the sixteenth-century's version of a bar association, responsible for the competence and moral probity of attorneys. In 1510, he was elected to Parliament and the office of Undersheriff of London, which meant that, among other prestigious and lucrative duties, he represented the City of London in the central court in Westminster. In this same period, he developed one of the largest and most profitable law practices in London by representing exporters of wool (Merchants of the Staple) and dealers in textiles

(Mercers' Company). In 1518, at age forty, More entered the king's service. By that time, he had already published *Utopia*, a hugely popular and influential work of humanism that would become an essential text of political philosophy. As a royal councilor, he filled a variety of judicial and executive positions (although the two were not always distinguished) under Henry VIII's Lord Chancellor, Cardinal Wolsey. For the next ten years, success followed success. After his knighthood in 1521, he received appointments that brought greater prestige and wealth: he was made speaker of the House of Commons in 1523 and Chancellor of the Duchy of Lancaster in 1525. The following year he was appointed to the Royal Council's subcommittee of four who oversaw all major concerns of the realm except war.

In 1526, the king began to suffer from a "scruple" concerning the validity of his marriage to Catherine of Aragon. The Queen had been previously married to his brother Arthur; but the marriage was never consummated and the union of

Catherine and Henry proceeded under a decree of nullity from the highest ecclesiastical court in Rome. At the same time, Henry was smitten by Anne Boleyn, while Catherine had not born him any sons. (Their sole, living issue was the future Queen Mary). It fell to the administrative genius, Cardinal Chancellor Wolsey, to gather expert opinions concerning the validity of Henry's marriage from the great universities of Europe and England. Then, in 1528, he shepherded the king's application for an annulment through a special tribunal convened in England. This was the "King's Great Matter."

It was only natural that Henry sought the opinion of his newest and closest advisor on this question. After requesting leave to study, More did not shrink from giving the king a disappointing answer. According to his biographer and son-in-law, William Roper, he "sought his Grace of sufficient respite advisedly to consider it," and undertook a study of Scripture and the Fathers of the Church. In the end he delivered a negative assessment, "which although the King . . . did not very well like of, yet were they by Sir Thomas More . . . so wisely tempered, that he both presently took them in good part, and oftentimes had thereof conference with him again."[1]

Henry's complacency did not last. In 1529, upon his return from a diplomatic mission on the Continent, Roper reports, "the King was as earnest in persuading Sir Thomas More to agree unto the matter of his marriage as before, by many and divers ways provoking him thereunto." On More's part, "he saw nothing of such force as could induce him to change his opinion therein."[2] It was also in 1529 that the king forced Cardinal Wolsey to resign, leaving the chancellor's office vacant. Wolsey fell from grace in 1529 for two reasons. First, England and France made peace at

---

1. William Roper, *The Life of Sir Thomas More, Knight* (hereinafter "Roper"), *A Thomas More Source Book*, ed. Gerard B. Wegemer and Stephen W. Smith (Washington, D.C.: Catholic University of America Press, 2004), 33. Hereinafter "*TMSB*."

2. Roper, *TMSB*, 32–34.

Cambrai, effectively ending Henry's dream—and the chancellor's overarching foreign policy—of (re-)claiming France. Second, Catherine stymied Wolsey's efforts to procure the annulment by successfully removing the King's Great Matter to Rome. The king decided to raise More, a layman, to the highest office in the realm.

Thus, when he was appointed chancellor, the annulment process was in a desperate stage for Henry; in Rome, the full influence of Catherine's nephew, Holy Roman Emperor Charles V, could be brought to bear. Nevertheless, More accepted the office. His position on the Great Matter was known to the king; and despite the repeated royal importuning to date, he remained firm. Now, at the pinnacle of power and prestige, More was "consulted" again by the king. Still unable to placate him, More fell back on the very advice which his sovereign imparted when he first entered royal service. After explaining how "grievous" it was not to be able to satisfy the king, More continued: "that [he] always bore in mind the most godly words that his Highness spake unto him at his first coming into his noble service . . . [that he willed] him first to look unto God, and after God to him . . . or else might his Grace well account him his most unworthy servant."[3] In this way, at the same time sincere and shrewd, idealistic and realistic, More enlisted the king's own words to defend himself against the king, even as he suggested that the royal policy ought to change.

Given our focus on More's heroic act of conscience, we are constrained to pass over any discussion of arguably the greatest achievement of More's tenure as chancellor, and to note only in passing the assessment of the great Tudor historian J. A. Guy: "He had added practical realism to Wolsey's idealism, and so ensured a smooth transition from the age of clerical to that of common-law chancellors. For thirty-one months in office, it was a magisterial performance."[4] Growing impatient with the delays

---

3. Roper, *TMSB*, 40.

4. John A. Guy, *The Public Career of Sir Thomas More* (New Haven: Yale University Press, 1980), 93.

and setbacks under traditional, ecclesiastical procedures of canon law, Henry decided to conscript Parliament, with the dogged and effective assistance of Thomas Cromwell, in reinventing the Church in England. Thus, in 1531, Henry was declared to be Supreme Head of the Church in England, albeit with a qualifier that bishops like John Fisher insisted upon—"'as far as the law of Christ allows.'"[5] The breaking point for More came, however, on May 15, 1532, with the Submission of the Clergy, under which the bishops of England relinquished their independence and ceded to the king and Parliament the ultimate authority to govern the English Church. (Leaving aside the historical and theological pretentions with which Henry sought to justify his Caesaropapism, Henry needed the Submission of the Clergy to give the English ecclesiastic court final say over his divorce and thereby disregard Catherine's appeal to Rome.)

---

5. Henry Ansgar Kelly, Louis W. Karlin, and Gerard B. Wegamer, eds., *Thomas More's Trial by Jury* (Woodbridge: The Boydell Press, 2011), 23.

On May 16, 1532, More resigned the chancellorship. He was willing to walk up to the edge of what was permissible in order to keep his position, satisfy the Crown, and influence policy. Indeed, as chancellor, he was called on to report the case in favor of the divorce to the House of Commons, specifically, to relate the favorable opinion from many centers of learning.[6] But, once Henry severed the English church from the papacy and the Catholic Church, and assumed those powers to himself, More could no longer serve. One year later, in May 1533, Archbishop Cranmer authorized the royal divorce. Anne Boleyn was crowned in June. Although invited and sent money for the

---

6. Guy corrects Roper. More did not resign until almost one year later, in May 1532, on the heels of the Submission of the Clergy. "The chancellor had been obliged to associate himself unquestionably with the king's policy. . . . Why then did More not resign [immediately before or after]? The answer lies in his convinced belief that the battle in Council could still be won; the Aragonese faction [i.e., the allies of Catherine of Aragon] was not conceding defeat in the spring of 1531." Guy, *Public Career of Sir Thomas More*, 158–159.

purchase of fitting attire for the event, More, at his peril, stayed home.[7]

FORMATION OF CONSCIENCE AND GIVING RIGHT SUBSTANTIAL COUNSEL

Loyal to his conscience, More withstood the king. "Henry's approval of [More's] appointment as Chancellor seems plainly to have rested partly on the miscalculation that he could win More around sooner or later to supporting the divorce."[8] Evidently, Henry underestimated his councilor's adherence to conscience. As Robert Bolt memorably put it, More did not have a "price." On the contrary, he courageously shared his honest assessment of the "Great Matter."

From where did More derive his confidence in such a consequential judgment? In the first place, he thought deeply about the need for good counsel. Second, he took great care in educating himself,

---

7. Roper, *TMSB*, 43–44.

8. Guy, *Public Career of Sir Thomas More*, 101.

or, informing his conscience, so that his advice and position on that question would be consistent with the truth. As he explained repeatedly, in letters from jail in the Tower of London, "for the instruction of my conscience I have not looked into this matter lightly, but have for many years given it serious study and consideration," which included the study of Sacred Scripture and the Church Fathers.[9] Of course, he had every incentive to do so. Rolling over was not an option. The matter implicated principles about the nature of marriage and had profound political implications. Of course, an answer in favor of divorce, or, more accurately, annulment, would save More and his family a world of trouble. More concluded, however, that the king's marriage to Catherine was valid. And he did not shy away from giving the king an answer—repeatedly—that Henry did not wish to hear. Informing the king of his conclusion, More went further than giving his opinion and fulfilling

---

9. Letter, August 1534, *TMSB*, 320.

an obligation to his sovereign and to the truth. He counseled Henry—diplomatically, of course—that neither he nor any of the members of his Council were qualified to be "counselors for your Grace herein" on account of the king's "manifold benefits daily bestowed on us so most bounden to you."[10] In this way, he was also imparting the benefit of a lifelong consideration, born of his study of classical authors, especially Cicero, of every man's need for "right substantial counsel." More appreciated the blinding effect of self-interest and the passions, which makes one an unreliable guide to advise oneself or another who effectively controls one's future. A king in the age before limited government was particularly vulnerable to self-deception, to the tendency to equate what he wanted with what was right. In addition to the corrupting influence of nearly untrammeled power, there was never a shortage of flatterers and unscrupulous social and political climbers. Consequently, upright advisors,

10. Roper, *TMSB*, 32.

as More aimed to be, played an especially critical role. Indeed, for this reason, following his resignation, More counseled Thomas Cromwell: "you are now entered into the service of a most noble, wise, and liberal prince; if you will follow my poor advice, you shall, in your counsel-giving unto His Grace, ever tell him what he ought to do. . . . So shall you show yourself a true faithful servant, and a right worthy Councillor. For if a lion knew his own strength, hard were it for any man to rule him."[11] It does not appear that Cromwell followed More's counsel. In any event, he did not fare better than More. Five years later, in late July 1540, he was beheaded for high treason.

In the end, however, the king was unmoved by More's opinion. In order to obtain legal sanction for the divorce and remarriage, he severed ties with the universal Church by forcing the Submission of the Clergy. More could no longer work for the Crown without cooperating in the evil—at

---

11. Roper, *TMSB*, 43.

least, as he saw it—that the king had visited on England. He resigned. By doing so, he embraced the loss of more than his own barge to take him to work at Westminster. He lost influence, power, prestige, and income to support his large family, a household of relatives, and servants, including tutors and a fool, on a grand estate.

SOURCES OF STRENGTH

The freedom of heart and courage required to relinquish the highest office in the realm and to risk the wrath of an absolute monarch were his first achievement. These qualities were obtained, above all, by a lifelong effort to cultivate a spiritual life, grounded in prayer and the Sacraments, but also in great learning, religious and, interestingly, secular.

After his resignation and refusal to attend Anne Boleyn's coronation, the Duke of Norfolk reminded More, "*indignatio principis mors est* [the anger of the king means death]." In response,

More quipped: "Is that all, my lord?. . . . Then in good faith is there no more difference between your Grace and me, but that I shall die today and you tomorrow."[12] In a similar manner, after resigning from office, he could joke about his loss of status. Evidently, while chancellor, after Sunday and holy day Masses, an attendant would tell his wife, Dame Alice, that her husband had left the church. "The next holy day after the surrender of his office and departure of his gentleman, he came unto my lady his wife's pew himself, and making a low curtsy, said unto her, 'Madame, my lord is gone.'"[13] (Whether Dame Alice appreciated the joke is another matter.) These anecdotes show a heart not set, in the first place, on the security derived from wealth and position, but one set on faith in God and his Providence.

So how did More achieve this freedom and courage of heart? The short answer is that More

---

12. Roper, *TMSB*, 50.

13. Ibid., 42.

was a saint—or, more accurately, struggling for holiness—before he was a martyr. He ordered his loves; he cultivated one love above all others, the love of God. To achieve this state of ordered loves, he maintained a robust spiritual life—prayer, penance, and sacraments—which aimed at constant growth in love of God. He practiced daily meditation, attended daily Mass, and went to weekly Confession. At Chelsea he constructed New House, which included a chapel. His penitential practices followed those lived in the strictest monasteries of his day, which included a hair shirt that he discreetly wore under the clothes befitting his high station in society.[14] More's very first published work, *Life of Pico* [*della Mirandola*], illustrates the importance which More gave to cultivating a spiritual life. It includes a reworking of a Renaissance love ballad, *Twelve Properties of a Lover*, into a love poem to God. It could only have been penned by someone with a deep, authentic piety:

---

14. Roper, *TMSB*, 40.

The first point is to love but one alone,
And for that one all others to forsake,
For whoso loveth many loveth none. . . .
So thou that hast thy love set unto God
In thy remembrance this imprint and grave:
As He in sovereign dignity is odd [i.e., unique],
So will He in love no parting fellows have.
Love Him therefore with all that He thee gave—
For body, soul, wit, cunning, mind and thought,
Part will He none, but either all or naught.[15]

Thus, from early on, he strove to put the love of God in the first place, in theory and in practice.

More's derived strength from reading: his study of the Bible, the Church Fathers, and the classics. His devotional, apologetic, and controversial writings show that he enjoyed a profound familiarity with the New Testament (including Erasmus' Greek-Latin translation, of course) and the Psalms. He also read many Church

---

15. *Twelve Properties of a Lover* (from *Life of Pico*), TMSB, 164.

Fathers, especially the Greek Fathers who had only recently become accessible to the men of the "new learning," such as More, who had mastered Greek. Undoubtedly, that steady diet of Holy Scripture and the Fathers served him well in the personal crisis occasioned by the King's Great Matter. More's readings were not limited to Scripture and the Fathers, however. From an early age and continuing through his legal studies and professional life, he studied classical literature (in the original, of course): poets, dramatists, historians, and philosophers, including Plato, Aristotle, Thucydides, Seneca, and Cicero. And he was unique among sixteenth-century northern humanists in stressing the importance of liberal studies for many, not just scholars. In defending the study of ancient Greek at Oxford University against those who complained that the pagan authors were unnecessary and antithetical to theology, More acknowledged that a person can be saved without secular learning—"and indeed without learning of any sort"—but he argued that classical studies taught "prudence in human affairs," adding, "[a]nd I doubt that any study contributes as richly to this practical skill as the study of the poets, orators, and histories."[16] Clearly, then, the authors of antiquity were a spiritual resource for More. In his *Dialogue Concerning Heresies*, a Socratic dialogue between More and a young man who has been swayed by Lutheran doctrine, More disputes the assertion that a Christian should not read beyond the Bible. A grounding in the liberal arts and an appreciation for great literature and should deepen one's grasp of Scripture. More was convinced, following St. Augustine's *De Doctrina Christiana* (*On Christian Teaching*), that, to understand Scripture, one must use reason.

> And just as the hand becomes the more
> nimble by the practicing of some feats, and
> the legs and feet the more swift and sure by

16. More, "Letter to the University of Oxford," in *Complete Works*, vol. 15 (New Haven: Yale University Press, 1987), 139; *see also* Wegemer, *Thomas More on Statesmanship*, 77.

habitual walking and running, and the whole body the more wieldy and healthy by some kind of exercise, so too there is no doubt that by study, effort, and exercise in logic, philosophy and the other liberal arts, reason is strengthened and invigorated.[17]

Contrary to the notion that poetry is merely "painted words," More argued that literary studies not only "help with the judgment," but they provide the "one special thing, without which all learning is half lame"—"a good mother wit."[18] By "mother wit," More meant a practical understanding of human reality in all its complexities and contradictions—how things really are, as opposed to what abstract reason might project.[19] Finally, More's sense of humor, demonstrated at his resignation as noted above, and present even in

17. More, *Dialogue Concerning Heresies*, rendered in modern English by Mary Gottschalk (New York: Scepter, 2006), 159.

18. Ibid., 159–160; *see also* Wegemer, *Thomas More on Statesmanship*, 11.

19. *See* Wegemer, *Thomas More on Statesmanship*, 82.

his most serious devotional writings, owed much to a central insight from classic texts: in order for a person's reason to rule over his passions, he must be capable of perceiving—and laughing at—human folly, especially his own. As Gerard Wegemer puts it, "literature can help shape civic behavior by assisting people to be more reflective and thus more deliberate in their actions. 'Powerful' literature shames ridiculous actions by artfully bringing them to light; it honors the noble and good in the same; it profoundly influences behavior by leading attentive readers to see the consequences of different ways of acting."[20]

MORE'S QUALIFIED EMBRACE OF THE WORLD

More was, at one and the same time, immersed in and apart from the world, a serpent and dove.[21] He appreciated created goods and grasped the

---

20. Ibid., 25.
21. Matt 10:16.

ways of the world. He could judge when it was no longer possible to engage with the world without offending God.

More's accession to the highest office in the realm illustrates this complex relationship with a radically imperfect world. More accepted the office of chancellor in the throes of the King's Great Matter. His decision was grounded in reasonable ambition and a concern for society. And he knew when he could pursue neither. This decision was not the result of naïveté or overweening ambition. He was keenly aware of the risks involved and set definite limits to his political goals.

Like his namesake in *Utopia*, More actively sought out public service in the royal court. As J. A. Guy says, "far from being the reluctant intellectual who manfully endured adversity, More instead, had steadily worked toward the goal of royal service"; it was, for him, "an act of positive, not negative motivation."[22] But his motivation

---

22. Guy, *Public Career of Sir Thomas More*, 7–9.

was not professional acclaim and financial rewards—indeed, his move to the public sector entailed a substantial loss of income, which it would take years to begin to recoup. More's views in this regard were much like those of Cicero, as expressed in his *De Officiis* (*On Obligations*): "while the acknowledging that a private life is typically easier and safer, a career of statecraft is more profitable to mankind and contributes more to their own greatness and renown."[23] Cicero argued that public service was an obligation for those "whom Nature has endowed with the capacity for administering public affairs" and he urged them to "put aside all hesitation, enter the race for public office, and take a hand in directing the government; for in no other way can a government be administered or greatness of spirit be made manifest."[24]

---

23. Cicero, *De Officiis*, 1.71, trans. Walter Miller (Cambridge, Mass.: Harvard UP, 1975).

24. Ibid.

In 1524, he moved from London to Chelsea in order to conduct official business. His home in the country commanded, in the words of Gerard Wegemer, "international fame."[25] It was a lordly manor after the fashion of the Renaissance. A famous sketch of More, Dame Alice, and their adult children by the German master Hans Holbein illustrates a household of learning, music, and piety. The presence of a clock and a pet monkey, musical instruments, and fine books and furnishings shows broad and good taste. Thus, More was in the world, very much in the world, but without being worldly. And, although he pursued wealth and position, he never lost sight of their transience.

An event in the life of the More family illustrates his Christian detachment. In 1529, at harvest time on the Chelsea estate, a fire destroyed More's barns, part of his home, and several of

---

25. Wegemer, *Thomas More: A Portrait of Courage* (Princeton: Scepter, 1995), 109.

the neighbors' barns. Lady Alice sent their son-in-law Giles Heron to inform More who, at the time, was away accompanying the king. While Heron waited, More, mindful probably of the teaching of the *Book of Job*, penned a letter to his wife, which started:

> And as I am informed by our son Heron of the loss of our barns and our neighbors' also with all the corn that was in them, except if it were not God's pleasure, it would be a great pity that so much good corn was lost. Yet since it has pleased him to send us such a chance, we must, and are bound, not only to be content, but also to be glad of his visitation. He sent us all that we have lost, and since he has by such a chance taken it away again, his pleasure be fulfilled; let us never grudge at it, but take it in good worth, and heartily thank him as well for adversity as for prosperity.[26]

---

26. Letter, September 3, 1529, *TMSB*, 180.

Further on, More also urged Alice "to make some good inquiry into what my poor neighbors have lost, and bid them take no thought of it for, even if I should not leave myself a spoon, there shall be no poor neighbor of mine who bears any loss because of an accident that happened in my house."[27]

The decision to become chancellor was not the result of worldly ambition. Like Cicero, he knew that a private life was safer and potentially more lucrative, but engagement in statesmanship was a virtue, if not a moral obligation, for those like him with a truly philosophical mindset. Despite this idealistic motivation, More was not naïve. He was acutely aware of the risks involved and set definite limits to political goals. In the world of kings and councilors, he understood, execution was an occupational hazard. The King's Great Matter merely heightened the usual risks attending royal service.

---

27. Ibid., 181.

Assuming the office of chancellor, he was seizing an opportunity to influence affairs in two positive ways. First and foremost, he could press the case in favor of Catherine of Aragon and the unity of the Catholic Church with the "indirect approach," which he explored in Book One of *Utopia*. Thanks to the scholarship of J. A. Guy, we can identify the various factions at work around the king from 1526 to 1532. When More was appointed Chancellor, the "Aragonese" party, the supporters of the Queen Catherine and Catholic unity, were locked in a struggle with allies of the Boleyn family, Lutherans, and other proto-Protestants.[28] (The Act of Submission of the Clergy marked the final defeat of Catherine's Aragonese party, whose success depended on the Queen's appeal to Rome.) In the second place, More could press ahead with the legal reforms that Wolsey had begun.

More's engagement with the world was the fruit of years of reflection, especially reflection on

---

28. Guy, *Public Career of Thomas More*, 138, 159.

the works of antiquity. Erasmus, the great human-
ist of northern Europe, wrote that "[c]ourt life
and the friendship of princes were formerly not
to [More's] taste, for he has always had a special
hatred of absolute rule and a corresponding love
for equality."[29] This dear friend was not resort-
ing entirely to convention. More's sayings and
writings evince an unflinching realism about the
prerogatives of princes; his understanding of how
political power tends to corrupt was drawn not
only from personal witness, but from his study of
Plato, Cicero, Seneca, and Augustine. In 1509,
young More, in a Coronation Ode on the occasion
of the accession of Henry VIII, wrote, "Unlimited power has a tendency to weaken good minds,
and that even in the case of very gifted men."[30]
Thus, he certainly harbored no illusions concerning the perils of working for a king. Roper once

29. "Erasmus on Thomas More," *TMSB*, 6. Quoted from a letter
written on July 23, 1519.

30. More, "Coronation Ode of King Henry VIII," *Center for
Thomas More Studies, http://www.thomasmorestudies.org//docs
/More_1509_Coronation_Ode.pdf.*

praised his father-in-law for the familiarity with which the king dealt with him. More responded, "I find his Grace my very good lord indeed, and I believe he doth as singularly favor me as any subject within this realm. Howbeit, son Roper, I may tell thee I have no cause to be proud thereof, for if my head could win him a castle in France (for then was there war between us) it should not fail to go."[31]

More not only recognized the depredations of princes, but he also thought deeply about the lives of rulers and their councilors and subjects. Immersed in the classical tradition, he appreciated the dangers of the rule of one. An early Latin poem, *On Lust for Power*, states: "Among many kings there will be scarcely one, if there is really one, who is satisfied to have one kingdom. And yet among many kings there will scarcely be one, if there is really one, who rules a single kingdom well."[32] Indeed, as a young man, he expressed a

---

31. Roper, *TMSB*, 27.

32. "On Lust for Power," *TMSB*, 239.

decided preference for representative government.[33] Among More's Epigrams, one finds this reflection on the "Best Form of Government":

> You ask which governs better, a king or a senate. . . . A senate would occupy a position between good and bad; but hardly ever will you have a king who is not either good or bad. An evil senator is influenced by advice from better men than he; but a king is himself the ruler of his advisers. A senator is elected by the people to rule; a king attains this end by being born. In the one case blind chance is supreme; in the other, a reasonable agreement. The one feels that he was made senator by the people; the other feels that the people

33. For More, genuine representative government was more than an instrument for foiling tyranny. It was, as Cicero explained in the last years of the Roman Republic, for citizens (not subjects) who work for the "maintenance of peace with dignity" in the commonwealth. For a scholarly treatment of More and his relationship with the political philosophers of antiquity, see Wegemer, *Young Thomas More and the Arts of Liberty* (New York: Cambridge University Press, 2011).

were created for him so that, of course, he may have subjects to rule.[34]

More was keenly aware of the ultimate absurdity of the world of kings.[35] No doubt he was wary of putting too much stock in the privileges of power: "And I wist [knew] once a great officer of the king's say—and in good faith, I ween [think] he

---

34. "Other Poems on Politics," *TMSB*, 237.

35. As a royal councilor, More attempted to mitigate the hazards of absolute power by finding a way to supply reliably to the king "right substantial counsel." In 1523, as Speaker of the House of Commons, he petitioned Henry VIII to grant "freedom of speech" to members of Parliament, the first such petition ever made and recorded:

> most gracious Sovereign, considering that in your high court of Parliament nothing is discussed but weighty and important matters concerning your realm and the your royal estate, many of your discreet commoners will be hindered from giving their advice and counsel, to the great hindrance of the common affairs, unless every one of your commoners is utterly discharged of all doubt and fear as to how anything that he happens to say may happen to be taken by Your Highness.

"Thomas More's 'Petition for Freedom of Speech,'" *TMSB*, 241. More should be credited with advancing a notion of freedom of speech as instrumental to good government.

said but as he thought—that twenty men standing
bareheaded before him kept not his head half so
warm as to keep on his own cap. Nor he took never
so much ease with their being bareheaded before
him . . . as he caught once grief with a cough
that came upon him by standing bareheaded
long [for a long time] before the king."[36] Elsewhere, More describes how death is democratic.
It exposes the illusory, deceptive nature of power,
especially the absolute power of monarchs. With
the literary aplomb which has secured his place
among the greatest writers of the English Renaissance, he imagined death coming to a king:

> there is no king so great but that . . . verily die
> he shall . . . and that himself, though he hope
> upon long respite of his execution—yet can he
> not tell how soon. And therefore, but if he be a
> fool, he can never be without fear that either on

---

36. *A Dialogue of Comfort Against Tribulation*, 221, Center for
Thomas More Studies, 2014, *https://thomasmorestudies.org/docs
/DialogueComfort2014-etext.pdf*.

the morrow or on the selfsame day, the grisly, cruel hangman Death . . . shall amidmong [in the midst of] all his royalty and all his main strength, neither kneel before him nor make him *any* reverence . . . nor with any good manner desire [ask] him to come forth . . . but rigorously and fiercely grip him by the very breast, and make all his bones rattle . . . and so, by long and diverse sore torments, strike him stark dead in this prison . . . and then cause his body to be cast into the ground in a foul pit within some corner of the same, there to rot and be eaten with wretched worms of the earth; sending yet his soul out further, unto a more fearful judgment.[37]

But, as we know, More did not scorn the world, despite its ultimate futility. Rather he engaged it. This theme of engagement is most apparent in Book One of *Utopia* (1515), which has been called the "Dialogue of Counsel," as well as in *The*

---

37. Ibid., 267–68.

History of Richard III (1513),[38] a historical-moral study of tyranny in the classical tradition. Both works were written in the period just before he entered the king's service.

The narrator in *Richard III* appreciates all that can go awry in the political world:

> And so they said that these matters be kings' games, as it were stage plays, and for the more part played upon scaffolds [i.e., a stage for play *and* platform for execution] in which poor men be but the lookers-on. And they that wise be, will meddle no farther. For they that sometimes step and play with them, when they cannot play their parts, they disorder the play and do themself no good.[39]

More's *History* does not suggest abandonment of the world, however, but virtuous engagement.

---

38. For probably political reasons, More left *The History of Richard III* unfinished.

39. Thomas More, *The History of Richard III*, modernized by George Logan (Bloomington: Indiana University Press, 2005), 95.

Thus, the *History* tells the story of how the abuse and neglect of law is a major force in the rise of tyranny. More does not make Richard's rise seem inevitable, much less providential. In the *History*, the lords and lawyers, as well as the commoners generally distinguish the good from the bad arguments. Nevertheless, power wins out because no one has the courage to stand up for the law and against the tyrant. Thus, by irony, or negative implication, we are left to imagine what might have happened if individuals had given force to the law to impede the tyrant's usurpation. More not only instructs readers on how to recognize would-be tyrants, but illustrates the tragic consequences of allowing tyranny to take root. We see repeatedly how Richard's adversaries underestimate his capacity for ruthless action.[40] The *History* also suggests another truth of political life, namely, that law is not sufficient for a just society.

---

40. See Karlin, "Law & Tyranny in More's *History of King Richard III*: An Examination of the Sanctuary Debate," *http://thomasmore studies.org/tmstudies/Karlin_RIII.pdf*.

Rather, integrity, personal virtue, is indispensable. Law without a virtuous citizenry is no match for the wiles of a would-be tyrant. Although for More "law is absolutely indispensable for the relative peace and justice of any society, law 'leaves many things to be pondered and weighed by [the judge's] wisdom.' Even the best laws can be abused."[41] Similarly, "Because the most basic cause of injustice arises from human nature itself and not from institutional structures. . . . No institutional arrangement, however, could withstand a corrupt citizenry."[42]

In Book One of *Utopia*, More, a character in his own dialogue, unsuccessfully attempts to persuade the philosopher-explorer-raconteur Raphael Hythloday why one should enter public service. Hythloday refuses to serve a king because "[t]here is no place for philosophy in the councils of kings." There, no one is concerned with truth,

---

41. Wegemer, *Thomas More on Statesmanship*, 69 (quoting *A Dialogue concerning Heresies*).

42. Ibid., 123.

morality or the common good, but only with getting and keeping power. More the interlocutor agrees in part, but argues that one is not therefore absolved from serving the public weal, for "there is another philosophy, better suited to the role of a citizen, that takes it cue, adapts itself to the drama at hand and acts its part neatly and appropriately." He recommends an "indirect approach" with more modest and realistic aims:

> That's how things go in the commonwealth, and in the councils of princes. If you cannot pluck up bad ideas by the root, or cure long-standing evils to your heart's content, you must not therefore abandon the commonwealth. Don't give up the ship in a storm because you cannot hold back the winds. . . . Instead, by an indirect approach, you must strive and struggle as best you can to handle everything tactfully—and thus what you cannot turn to good, you may at least make as little bad as possible.[43]

43. Thomas More, *Utopia*, ed. George Logan and Robert Adams (Cambridge: Cambridge University Press, 2002), 34–35.

Thus, More was not put off by the compromises that life in royal service entailed. But he strove to make engagement with the world compatible with eternal destiny. His understanding that life in the world meant playing roles, as in a play, along with his endorsement of an "indirect approach" when applying philosophic truths to human action, capture his belief in the transience and *ultimate* unreality of life in the world. As a student and close reader of St. Augustine, especially *City of God*, More was careful not to attempt to advocate, much less work to impose, a celestial kingdom on earth of sinless humans. He was equally careful not to abandon himself to worldly ambition and carnal desire. Rather, he embodied *integrity*. He was at the very top of the legal profession and a man of prayer and penance—Lord Chancellor wearing a hair shirt under his rich gown and chain of office. Thus, he could accept a powerful, prestigious government position, mindful of the effectiveness, and the limits, of the "indirect approach." Those limits pertained not merely to the hazards of persuading a king to do what is right, but also to the ethical restraints that More imposed on his association with the Crown.

The Submission of the Clergy, however, marked the end of that engagement. With no right of appeal to Rome, the Aragonese party was routed. The English Church surrendered its independence to the Crown and left the jurisdiction of the universal Church. More recognized that he could no longer play the "role" of counselor, and that the "indirect approach" could no longer be employed without cooperating in the evils perpetrated by the king and Parliament. Drawing on the deep spiritual reserves built up during a lifetime of holy living, he acted in consequence of the truth as he perceived it and resigned.

CHAPTER 3

Oath of Succession and More's Imprisonment

HISTORICAL AND LEGAL BACKGROUND

On April 17, 1534, More was arrested for refusing to swear the Oath of Succession three days earlier. The oath was imposed in connection with the Act of Succession (March 1534), a statute which legitimated the marriage of Henry and Anne Boleyn and recognized Anne as queen and their offspring as heirs to the throne. In his first letter from the Tower, he left a record that he was ready to swear to the succession but could not swear the oath, as presented, without violating his conscience: "[T]hough I would not deny to swear to the succession, yet unto the oath that there was offered me I could not swear without iubarding [i.e., jeopardizing] of my soul to perpetual damnation."[1] In November 1534, he was convicted by bill of attainder, that is, without trial, but by an act of Parliament.[2]

The Oath of Succession penalized refusal to swear as misprision of treason, a lesser offense to high treason. Accordingly, More was sentenced to life in prison and confiscation of all his property—the maximum penalty for misprision of treason (as opposed to the capital offense of high treason). There is no record of the exact contents of the oath administered to More. Nevertheless, we know why he was prepared to go to jail and lose his property. After reading the oath for the first time, he objected that it went

---

1. Letter, April 17, 1534, *TMSB*, 312.

2. About 250 years later, the United States Constitution forbade bills of attainder for both the states and the federal government. U.S. Constitution, art. I, § 9.

beyond the terms of the Act itself, which (only) legitimated the succession through the new queen.[3] It effectively commanded approval of the English Church's break with Rome, as well. Subsequently, and perhaps in response to More's refusal and complaint that the oath exceeded the fact of royal succession, Parliament passed an act legislating the contents of the oath. The oath as approved by act of Parliament indeed required each person to swear to more than the succession, that is, that Anne and her progeny are rightful rulers: "you shall observe, keep, maintain, and defend the said Act of Succession, and all the whole effects and contents thereof, *and all other Acts and statutes made in confirmation*, or for the execution of the same, or of anything therein contained. . . ."[4] At this point, there were already a number of anti-Catholic statutes, including the Act of Submission of the Clergy and Restraint

3. Letter, 17 April 1534, *TMSB*, 312.

4. The First Act of Succession, A.D. 1534, 25 Henry VIII, CAP. 22. (*Statutes of the Realm* 3:471–4).

of Appeals (1534), Peter's Pence and the Submission of the Clergy (1532), which had trig-
gered More's resignation of office. Thus, the oath
administered to More embraced the independence of the English Church from the universal Church, at least to the extent that sealing off
the governance of the local Church from Rome
entailed severing her allegiance to the universal
Church. Thus, More's arrest and conviction for
misprision of treason is of one piece with his resignation of office. He suffered in both instances
for the unity of the Church and for refusing to
cooperate in the rupture of the "common corps of
Christendom," in the English crown's arrogation
of unprecedented ecclesial authority.[5]

---

5. More's adherence to the unity of Christendom implied loyalty to
the pope as a supreme pastor *of souls*. He distinguished between the
spiritual and temporal prerogatives of the papacy. Only the former
commanded his allegiance; international politics was another matter.
In fact, as a royal councilor, he cautioned Henry (in vain) not to ally
the country too closely with the papacy. Letter to Cromwell, March
5, 1534, in *St. Thomas More: Selected Letters,* ed. Elizabeth Frances
Rogers (New Haven, Ct.: Yale University Press, 1967), 212. More
stood for the integrity and independence of secular realm.

Nature of Refusal:
Principled and Tactical

More's refusal was an exercise of the "indirect approach." It took into account several competing goals in a complex balancing. Refusing the oath was the least dangerous course. It allowed More to remain faithful to his conscience and witness to the truth while containing the wrath of the Crown. (To condemn openly the oath was to invite prosecution for treason and commit the sin of presumption by courting martyrdom.) More also had a high regard for the rule of law. An act of civil disobedience was a decision that cut against his instincts and required careful consideration.

To swear falsely was out of the question for More. Still, he had not given up on saving his life. He explained to the royal councilors administering the oath:

> I feared lest the King's Highness would as they said take displeasure enough toward me for only the refusal of the oath. And that if I

should open and disclose the causes why, I should therewith but further exasperate his Highness, which I would in no wise do, but rather would I abide all the danger and harm that might come toward me, than give his Highness any occasion of further displeasure that the offering of the oath unto me of pure necessity constrained me.[6]

Amid competing obligations—to his family, himself, the Church, the country and (we should not forget) Catherine of Aragon—More cut a cautious, conservative course. Clearly, he was not in favor of casting aside Queen Catherine; he had applied all his wits to averting such an outcome. Yet he was ready to sign on to the succession because, while it was unjust and unwise, it was not a *malum in se*, i.e., a wrong in itself, but touched a matter entrusted to Parliament.

False swearing, however, was another matter. It implicated a moral absolute. Again, he could

---

6. Letter, April 17, 1534, *TMSB*, 313.

not swear the oath without jeopardizing his soul. More counter-offered to take an oath swearing that he did not refuse for any other reason than "to swear it was against my conscience;" but his accusers declined.[7] Thus, he was heeding the call of truth, following his conscience. At the same time, he aimed to head off a charge of high treason, while perhaps anticipating the next step of Henry and Cromwell. His bare refusal of the oath meant punishment of life in prison and confiscation of goods for misprision of treason; but to avoid exacerbating his circumstances, he repeatedly claimed: "I never withdrew any man from [taking the oath], nor never advised any to refuse it, nor never put, nor will, any scruple in any man's head, but leave every man to his own conscience."[8]

For More, failure to comply with the king and Parliament was actually a rare case wherein one

_____

7. Ibid.

8. Ibid., 315.

could, without offending God, refuse to follow
the law:

> I thought myself I might not well do so [i.e.
> swear to the succession], because that in my
> conscience this was one of the cases in which
> I was bounden that I should not obey my
> prince, sith [since] that whatsoever other folk
> thought in the matter (whose conscience and
> learning I would not condemn nor take upon
> me to judge), yet in my conscience the truth
> seemed on the other side.[9]

Mindful of the fragility of public order, More
keenly felt the obligation to obey lawful public
authority. Familiar with classical history and
England's recent civil war, which put Henry
VIII's father on the throne, he cultivated a high
regard for the rule of law; it was a bulwark
against tyranny and—equally dreaded—anarchy.
He famously told his son-in-law, "Were it my

---

9. Ibid., 314.

father on the one side and the devil on the other, his cause being good, the devil should have his right."[10]

During one of her visits to the Tower, Margaret argued that her father was, "under pain of losing [his] soul, bound to . . . reform [his] conscience to other men's" precisely because it "is commanded by Parliament."[11] More responded that individual conscience actually trumps the law of the land—although one does not avoid suffering the consequences of civil disobedience:

> But, Margaret, first, as for the law of the land, though everyone born in and inhabiting it is bound to keep it in every case under pain of some temporal punishment, and in many cases also under pain of God's displeasure,

---

10. Roper, *TMSB*, 36.

11. Letter from Margaret Roper to Alice Alington, August 1534, *TMSB*, 328. This Tower letter is believed to be jointly authored by More and his daughter Margaret.

still no one is bound to swear that every law is well made, or bound under pain of God's displeasure to perform any point of the law that is actually unlawful.[12]

In fact, during his incarceration, More examined his justification for disregarding the law. He explicitly reviewed his understanding of oath taking, recalling that "perjury is a violation of a *lawful* oath. Otherwise, he who swears to kill someone, would sin if he did not kill."[13] In other words, one is not bound to obey an unlawful law. Thus, in refusing an oath demanded by an illicit law, More's conscience was informed by a deep tradition, summarized in the *Summa Theologiae* of St. Thomas Aquinas, that "if . . . the judge asks of [the accused] that which he cannot ask in accordance with the order of justice, the accused

---

12. Ibid.

13. *The Yale Edition of the Complete Works of Thomas More*, ed. John Guy et al., vol. 6 (New Haven, Ct.: Yale University Press, 1987), 765–67; emphasis added.

is not bound to satisfy him, and he may lawfully escape by appealing or otherwise; but it is not lawful for him to lie."[14] For More, it was lawful to refuse the oath only because he considered it to exceed lawful limits. This narrow case of conscience did not entitle him to an exemption by the state or reprieve from punishment, however. More's conduct was an act of defiance only accidently; defiance was a foreseeable but not necessarily intended consequence of his action. His decision to refuse the oath was undertaken cautiously, not just on account of the danger of further prosecution, but also because of his regard for the rule of law.

COURAGE IN FOLLOWING THE JUDGMENT OF CONSCIENCE

One aspect of More's achievement in refusing to take the Oath of Succession lies in his courage

---

14. Aquinas, *Summa Theologiae* 2–2.69.1.

in the face of overwhelming social pressure. It is hard to overestimate how alone he was. And who has not experienced the second-guessing and doubts upon finding oneself without an ally? Still, More never lost sight of the personal nature of the judgment of conscience.

In April 1534, More was the only layman called to swear the oath, and one of the very few who refused. Following his incarceration, he wrote numerous letters to his daughter Margaret; these meticulously drafted communications were intended not only for her and his family, but also for a larger audience, indeed for posterity. In the first one, More noted his isolation, observing: "I somewhat marveled in my mind, considering that they sent for no more temporal men but me."[15] Indeed, the entire political and spiritual leadership of England abandoned More. Every royal councilor and every bishop in England, bar one, John Fisher of Rochester, swore the oath. Thus,

---

15. Letter, April 17, 1534, *TMSB*, 312.

More was almost alone in his decision among the English elite, his social and political equals. Furthermore, among his family members, no one, not even his beloved daughter Margaret, supported his decision. Indeed, they urged him to take the oath. In letters to her father in prison, Margaret advanced several lines of argument to persuade him to swear. Not entirely joking, More, referred to his beloved daughter as "Mistress Eve."[16] Undoubtedly, her letters increased the moral suffering involved in watching his family pay the price of his decision—their loss of father/husband and income.[17] How confounding it must have been for More to sacrifice so much over a matter

16. It is possible, in light of the elaborate care that went into More's Tower letter, that Margaret was "presented" as opposed to her father to supply More a device for presenting the arguments against his decision. On the other hand, in light of the landslide in favor of the Oath of Succession, it would not be surprising if she actually urged her father to take the oath with a "reservation."

17. Land, home, and goods were prudently transferred before April 1534, but with limited success.

that did not trouble any, or practically any, of his contemporaries.

Efforts to dissuade More from refusing to take the oath came from the highest levels of society. His daughter conveyed this message from Lord Audley, the new chancellor: "whereas you say your conscience moves you to do this, all the nobles of this realm, and almost all other men too, are boldly going forth with the contrary, with no hesitation, excepting only yourself and one other man [Fisher]."[18] But "companionship," the society of his fellows, even for the man who was famous for his wit and bonhomie, did not sway him in a matter in which his soul was hanging in the balance. More explained to Margaret that if the bishops and other royal councilors follow their consciences and swear, and he, "for companionship's sake go[es] along with them" and swears against his conscience, "in judgment at the bar

---

18. Letter from Margaret Roper to Alice Alington, August 1534, *TMSB*, 321.

before the high Judge," God will "[send] them to heaven and [More] to the devil." Companionship will not save him. Rather:

> if I should then say . . . , "My old good lords and friends," naming such-and-such a lord—yes, and perhaps some of the bishops I love best—"I swore because you swore, and went the way that you went; now do the same for me; don't let me go alone; if there be any good fellowship among us, some of you come with me," upon my honor, Margaret, . . . among them all I think I would find not one who would for good fellowship go to the devil with me.[19]

In the same vein, he told his daughter the story of "Company," the single hold-out juror. "Are there not eleven of us here and you just one? . . . Play then the good companion. Come along with us on that basis; go ahead, just as good company."

19. Ibid., *TMSB*, 325–28.

"Company" responds: "[W]hen we depart and come before God, and he sends you to heaven for doing according to your conscience, and me to the devil for doing against mine . . . [will you] go with me now [to hell] to keep me good company . . . ?"[20] The famously social More endured isolation and opposition from his peers by drawing ever closer to the relationship which mattered most.

More appreciated that one's relationship with God is mediated by conscience. And, ultimately, everyone is alone in the decision of his conscience. He had to decide for himself in light of the truth of revelation and reason, not popular opinion: "And since in this matter I look only to God, it matters little to me if men call it as it pleases them and say it is not a matter of conscience but just a foolish scruple."[21] He was also aware of the ways

20. Ibid. *TMSB*, 326–27.

21. Letter from Margaret Roper to Alice Alington, August 1534, *TMSB*, 320.

in which conscience is compromised by crisis. In the same exchange, More questioned whether everyone rushing to swear had remained true to his conscience and, for that reason, More refused to "pin [his] soul to another man's back":

Some might do something for favor, and some might do it for fear, and so they might carry my soul a wrong way. And some might happen to frame themselves a conscience and think that as long as they did it for fear, God would forgive it. And some may perhaps think that they will repent and be absolved of it, and so God will remit it. And some may perhaps be thinking that if they say one thing while thinking the contrary, God more regards their heart than their tongue, and that therefore their oath goes by what they think and not by what they say, as a woman reasoned once.[22] . . . But

22. More was referring to his wife, Dame Alice, or his daughter, Margaret.

honestly, Margaret, I can use no such ploys in so great a matter.[23]

Quibbling?

The refusal to take the Oath of Succession was an exacting exercise of conscience. It was not only courageous, but clear-sighted. With all that he had to give up by going to prison, we can take More at his word that "[t]here is no man who has taken the oath already who has done so more gladly than I would," if his conscience did not forbid it.[24] More had to confront the possibility that he went to prison and ruined his family for a quibble. The Crown was accusing him of "obstinacy." "Allies" and "friends" were certain that he had fallen prey to "scrupulosity." Both assessments were at least defensible. In the early sixteenth century, before the Council of Trent, it was not certain

---

23. Letter from Margaret Roper to Alice Alington, August 1534, *TMSB*, 325.

24. Ibid., 320.

that the unity of Christendom required an appeal to Rome. For this reason, among more compelling ones to be sure, like avoiding sedition, More was loathe to condemn others who had sworn: "Howbeit (as help me God), as touching the whole oath, I never withdrew any man from it, nor never advised any to refuse it, nor never put, nor will, any scruple in any man's head, but leave every man to his own conscience."[25] The point at stake was not obvious, but required study and even foresight. In contrast, from More's historical vantage point, no one could have reasonably agreed that a king could make himself the head of the Church. Even in the East, where Caesaropapism was well-established since the fourth century, no secular lord had the cheek to claim immediate, direct jurisdiction over the church, as Henry, through Parliament, was to do in December 1534 with the Act of Supremacy (passed while More was in prison). But as long as his imprisonment rested on a violation of the

---

25. Letter, April 17, 1534, *TMSB*, 315.

Oath of Succession, he had to exact a remarkable degree of honesty to stay loyal to a conclusion at which so few had arrived.[26]

From prison, in correspondence, More confronted the possibility that he was suffering from a case of scruples. Lord Audley, again through Margaret, in a friendly, cajoling manner urged More to get over his oversensitive conscience. He entrusted her with a "merry tale" about a lion, a wolf, and an ass who go to confession to Father Fox. In the tale, the ass accuses himself of taking one straw from his master's shoe for hunger and that because of this he thinks his master had caught a cold. "His confessor could not absolve this great trespass, but immediately sent him to the bishop." But the lion receives absolution straightaway for devouring all the beasts "on grounds that he is king and also that it was his nature so to do." Finally, the wolf also gets absolved without delay

---

26. Even the Carthusian monks of the Charterhouse, who were later martyred for refusing to acknowledge the King as Supreme Head of the Church, took the Oath of Succession.

for gluttony and devises an end-run around his penance not to eat more than a sixpence of food at any one meal. He reasons his way to valuing a tasty-looking cow at four pence.

> But when the wolf had been on this diet a little while, he grew very hungry. So much so that one day, when he saw come by him a cow with her calf, he said to himself, 'I am very hungry and would gladly eat, except that I am bound by my spiritual father. Well, notwithstanding that, my conscience must be my judge. So, then if that be so, my conscience will be thus: that the cow does not seem to me to be worth but four pence, then the calf is worth but two pence.' And so the wolf ate both of the cow and the calf.[27]

More observed in a subsequent letter how the wolf "enlarges his conscience."[28] To More, this

27. Letter from Alice Alington to Margaret Roper, August 1534, *TMSB*, 318.

28. Letter from Margaret Roger to Alice Alington, August 1534, *TMSB*, 324.

was an ever-present danger when moral obligations conflict with public pressure or personal
desire. To be sure, he got the point of Audley's
tale: "my scrupulous conscience is taking for a
huge danger to my soul something that my Lord-
ship thinks in reality be but a trifle: namely, if I
were to take this oath."[29] But, he was content to
appear as the seemingly scrupulous ass and suffer
the scorn of his contemporaries, rather than yield
to his fears and jeopardize his salvation.

SUSTAINING HIS RESOLVE

En route to Lambeth, where he was to refuse the
oath and trigger his arrest on misprision of treason, More famously told his son-in-law Roper: "I
thank Our Lord, the field is won."[30] If his statement perplexed Roper, More's import is clear
from our vantage point: he had settled on his
course of action with a clear conscience. From

---

29. Ibid. *TMSB*, 324.

30. Roper, *TMSB*, 51.

prison, More exclaimed in writing to his daughter that he would not change his mind concerning the oath "even if I should see my Lord of Rochester [John Fisher] . . . take the oath himself, right in front of me."[31] His conscience overcame the pain of losing family, property, and liberty. Yet, More struggled, literally, with all his mind and imagination, to stay the course. Before his arrest, he began writing a *Treatise on the Passion*, steeling himself for an approaching storm. In that work, which he finished in prison, he wrote: "All that we ever have, from God we have received—riches, status, authority, beauty, strength, learning, intelligence, body, soul, and all. And almost all these things he has only lent us. For we must depart again from every last one of these things, except our soul alone. And that, too, we must give back to God, or else we shall keep it forever with such sorrow that we would be better off losing it."[32] He was

31. Letter from Margaret Roper to Alice Alington, August 1534, *TMSB*, 325.

32. *Treatise on the Passion, TMSB*, 217–18.

preparing himself to persevere through the shame and pain of incarceration and possible execution.

And then, once in prison, in labors of great literary merit, in *A Dialogue of Comfort against Tribulation* and *The Sadness of Christ*, he plumbed the sources of strength to be faithful in the face of tribulation. *Dialogue of Comfort* is a lengthy, imaginary conversation in three separate books. Although More sets the narrative in a faraway country, his careful contemporary readers would not miss the parallels to England under Henry VIII. For readers today, the concerns are frighteningly immediate. The *Dialogue* takes place in Hungary, between an older man, Anthony, and his nephew, Vincent. The Turk threatens to sack their city; by Book Three the attack is imminent; and the Christians face loss of property and life unless they forsake their religion.

Sadness is a meditation on Christ's agony in the garden. It picks up after the Last Supper and ends at Christ's arrest. Although the focus of the work and its originality center on the ways in which Christ inspires and comforts reluctant, fearful martyrs like More himself, there are profound contemporary historical insights: only the most obtuse clerics of the time would have failed to see themselves in More's portrait of the sleeping Apostles. These works leave no doubt as to More's source of strength: meditation on Christ in his Passion, suffering, and conquering of fear and pain. He was convinced that Christ suffered not only to remit sins, but also to quicken his followers to accept suffering.

> When it comes to bearing a loss of worldly goods and suffering captivity, enslavement, and imprisonment, and gladly sustaining worldly shame, if we would on all those points deeply ponder the example of our Savior himself, this by itself would be enough to encourage every warm-blooded Christian, whether man or women, never to refuse to suffer for his sake any or all of those calamities. And now I say the same for a painful death. If only

we could and would with due compassion conceive in our minds a right imagination and remembrance of Christ's bitter, painful Passion![33]

It merits repeating that More was striving for holiness before his incarceration. The so-called Tower Works disclose the richness of his spiritual life, the depth of his relationship with God.

This fact is the key to his heroic perseverance *in extremis*. In *A Dialogue of Comfort*, More forcefully and humorously rejects the notion of deathbed conversion; one should expect to die as one lives.

They tell of one that was wont always to say that all the while he lived he would do what he list . . . for three words when he died should make all safe enough. But then so happed it that long ere he were old, his horse

33. "More's Conception of God," from *A Dialogue of Comfort against Tribulation* in *TMSB*, 261.

once stumbled upon a broken bridge; and as he labored to recover him, when he saw it would not be . . . but down into the flood headlong needs he should . . . in a sudden flight he cried out in the falling, 'Have all to the devil!' And there was he drowned, with his "three words ere he died" whereon his hope hung all his wretched life.[34]

More entered the Tower already fortified by the strength of grace. There was no improvising. He was prepared for the crisis because every day he was trying to put God first. Thus, despite the blinding pressures of isolation and loss of freedom, conscience reliably guided his actions toward the good and the true, despite the overwhelming cost.

---

34. *A Dialogue of Comfort against Tribulation*, 92, (CTMS ed., 2013).

CHAPTER 4

Act of Supremacy and More's Trial and Execution

HISTORICAL AND LEGAL BACKGROUND

More suspected that the Crown would not settle for life in prison or pass up an opportunity to change the mind of this high-profile prisoner. Margaret reminded him that "Master Secretary [Cromwell] sent you word, as your true friend [!], to remember that Parliament is still in session." More was unfazed:

> I thank him with all my heart. But as I explained to you then, I have not failed to think about that. And although I know well that if they were to make a law designed to do

me harm, that law [which Parliament would soon enact, namely, the Treasons Act of 1534] could never be lawful, and I trust God will so keep me in grace that concerning my duty to my king, no man will be able to hurt me without doing me wrong (and then, as I told you, this is like a riddle, a case in which a man may lose his head and not be harmed). . . .[1]

From the outset, then, he knew that he was risking more than life in prison and confiscation of goods. Indeed, as he related in one of his letters to Margaret, "I have, before I came here, not failed to think of and ponder the very worst and absolute most that can possibly happen."[2] The "very worst and absolute most" did come to pass. Toward the end of 1534, after six months in jail, More faced, not just hardship from loss of liberty, goods, and reputation, but death as a traitor. Parliament

1. Letter from Margaret Roper to Alice Alington, August 1534, *TMSB*, 333.
2. Ibid., 320.

passed the Act of Supremacy, declaring the king Supreme Head of the Church in England, as well as the Treasons Act, making it high treason to "maliciously" deprive the king of his title, punishable by hanging, drawing, and quartering. Armed with those new statutes, Thomas Cromwell and other royal councilors commenced interrogations of More, ordering him to affirm the king's newly-minted title. More's reports of these encounters display his characteristic wit and irony. His objective, legalistic description of the new law implicitly highlights what he undoubtedly understood to be a radical revision of England's traditions: since "it was now by act of Parliament ordained that his Highness and his heirs be, and ever right have been, and perpetually should be Supreme Head in the earth of the Church of England under Christ, the king's pleasure was that those of his council should demand mine opinion, and what my mind was therein."[3] Over the course

---

3. Letter, May 2, 1535, *TMSB*, 344.

of three interrogations dealing with the royal supremacy, More refused to answer, employing a defense of silence:

> I give no man occasion to hold any one point or the other, nor never any man advise or counsel therein one way or another. And for conclusion I could no further go, whatsoever pain should come thereof. I am, said I, the King's true faithful subject and daily beadsman and pray for his Highness and all his and all the realm . . . And therefore my poor body is at the King's pleasure; would God my death might do him good.[4]

On June 26, 1535, he was indicted for violating the Treasons Act. On July 1, 1535, he was tried and convicted of high treason and sentenced to be hanged, drawn, and quartered.[5] He was executed—beheaded—on July 6, 1535. (The

4. Ibid., 344–46.

5. For a study of the trial, see *Thomas More's Trial by Jury*, eds. H. A. Kelly et al.

Crown mitigated the punishment, probably in exchange for a promise to make his final statement on the scaffold a short one.) The king's councilors attempted several times during his fifteen-month imprisonment to gather evidence. The evidence mainly consisted of "obstinate silence," that is, refusal to answer the questions of Thomas Cromwell and other interrogators concerning the king's marriage and new title. Again, it bears emphasizing that all of these refusals occurred during his Tower interrogations in April, May, and June 1535, which were *after* he had been convicted of violating the Act of Succession by refusing its oath and *after* the passage of the Acts of Supremacy and Treasons. Evidence at trial also included the exchange between him and Richard Rich, which occurred on June 12, 1535, and concerned whether More disclosed his long-concealed opinion that Parliament had no legitimate authority to make Henry the Supreme Head of the English Church. Finally, he was also convicted on the basis of letters exchanged with fellow-martyr John Fisher, Bishop of Rochester, who was tried, convicted, and executed ten days before the start of More's trial. At trial, we know that More argued—likely, in a post-trial motion to dismiss the indictment as insufficient as a matter of law[6]—that the indictment was "invalid as contrary to God's laws and those of the Church and England, as a small part of the Church, should not make a law which was at odds with the general law ecclesiastical." He also asserted that the Act of Supremacy was contrary to *Magna Carta* and the Coronation Oath, both of which guaranteed the independence of the Church.[7]

CIVIL LAW AND CONSCIENCE

In the sixteenth century, defendants did not enjoy a right against self-incrimination. By refusing to

---

6. For an insightful discussion of post-verdict events, see Kelly, "A Procedural Review of Thomas More's Trial," in *Thomas More's Trial by Jury*, 41.

7. Roper, *TMSB*, 59–60.

answer Cromwell and the Crown's other representatives, More arguably put himself outside the law. Undoubtedly he was aware that "the accused is in duty bound to tell the judge the truth which the latter exacts from him according to the form of law. Hence if he refuse to tell the truth which he is under obligation to tell . . . he sins mortally."[8] Indeed, Thomas Audley, the new chancellor, and Master Secretary Cromwell advised More "that the king might by his laws compel [him] to make a plain answer thereto, one way or the other." More did not disagree but responded that he "would not dispute the King's authority." Nevertheless, as he went on to explain, "the case seemed . . . somewhat hard to say precisely with it against my conscience to the loss of my soul, or precisely against it to the destruction of my body."[9] More, in refusing to answer his interrogators, was thinking of the narrow exception to the rule,

---

8. Aquinas, *Summa Theologiae* 2–2.69.1.

9. Letter, June 3, 1535, *TMSB*, 349.

discussed above, that in certain, limited cases, it is lawful to withhold the truth: "a man is not bound to divulge all truth, but only such as the judge can and must require of him according to the order of justice."[10] Disobedience to the civil law was permitted because the law was unjust. Arrogation of the universal Church's authority by a secular ruler of a local church (England) was indefensible.

Furthermore, it violated the fundamental rights and liberties of English citizens, as expressed in *Magna Carta* and the Coronation Oath. For these reasons, he judged it his responsibility not to follow an unlawful law but to follow his conscience. Thus, More stood for the proposition that the civil law is never beyond reasoned judgment in accordance with natural and divine law. Where positive law conflicts with divine law, conscience requires conformity to the true law.

This was not the position of the Crown. Cromwell, in particular, insisted that More must

---

10. Aquinas, *Summa Theologiae* 2–269.2.

conform his conscience to the law of the realm. Despite his fundamental disagreement with that position, More did not assume that the state was obliged to change the law or grant an accommodation for the individual conscience. For More, who followed Cicero in the understanding that respect for the law was essential to ensure civil order and personal liberty, it was remarkable enough that civil disobedience was permissible at all. The overriding moral duty to follow one's conscience might entail profound hardship: "as for the law of the land, though everyone born in and inhabiting it is bound to keep it in every case under pain of some temporal punishment, and in many cases under pain of God's displeasure, still no one is bound to swear that every law is well made, or bound under pain of God's displeasure to perform any point of the law that is actually unlawful."[11] Conscience, then, did

---

11. Letter from Margaret Roper to Alice Alington, August 1534, *TMSB*, 328–29.

not mitigate the coercive effect of the law, for "everyone . . . is bound to keep [the law] in every case under pain of some temporal punishment." Rather, a conflict between God's law and man's results in a limited license to disobey (and accept the punishment for disobedience), for no one is bound to endorse every law, or bound to perform any point of the law that is "actually unlawful."[12] This explains why More characterized Henry's new statute as a "double-edged sword,"[13] and what More meant by losing one's head and suffering no harm.[14]

DEFENSE OF SILENCE

More's silence was not an assertion against self-incrimination. It was a legally and morally acceptable tactic, the best available defense against

---

12. Ibid., 328–29.

13. *Paris Newsletter's Account, TMSB,* 352.

14. Letter from Margaret Roper to Alice Alington, August 1534, *TMSB,* 333.

tyranny and an unjust law. In fact, More had employed silence earlier in his career. During his tenure as Speaker of the House of Commons, More defended the liberty of the House by counseling "silence" before the demands of the Crown, anticipating his own response to the Royal Supremacy. In an attempt to force the passage of "a very great subsidy," the chancellor, Cardinal Wolsey, violated longstanding custom by appearing in person in the House of Commons "with his whole train." After his speech Wolsey demanded "some reasonable answer." When the House members responded by holding their peace, the chancellor accused them of "a marvelous obstinate silence" and demanded "an answer of Master Speaker." More, who "first reverently upon his knees excusing the silence of the House [showed] that for them to make answer was it neither expedient nor agreeable with the ancient liberty of the House. . . ."[15] In connection with

15. Roper, *TMSB*, 26.

the Act of Supremacy, silence was "expedient." By strictly keeping his own counsel and refusing to answer the royal examiners, More lawfully deprived his opponents of evidence of sedition and, thus, the right to question him.[16]

More's silence was also consistent. He repeatedly insisted with interrogators that "I meddle not with the conscience of them that think otherwise."[17] According to the Paris Newsletter account of More's trial (August 4, 1535), it was only after his conviction that More addressed directly the merits of the case. With respect to the principal charge of high treason for denying the king's new title, he replied he could not be condemned to death for "such silence, for neither your Statute nor any laws in the world punish people except for words or deed—surely not for keeping silence." The prosecutor countered that "such silence was certain proof of malice intended against the statute,

---

16. In addition, by not boldly pronouncing against the king's new title he was avoiding the sin of presumption.

17. *E.g.*, Letter, June 3, 1535, *TMSB*, 350.

especially as every faithful subject, on being questioned about the statute, was obliged to answer categorically that the Statute was good and wholesome." "Surely," More replied:

> "if what the common law says is true, that he who is silent seems to consent, my silence should rather be taken as approval than contempt of your Statute. You say that all good subjects are obliged to reply; but I say that the faithful subject is more bound to his conscience and his soul than to anything else in the world, *provided his conscience, like mine, does not raise scandal or sedition*, and I assure you that never discovered I what is in my conscience to any person living."[18]

More's qualification of his insistence on conscience— that it caused neither scandal nor sedition— deserves careful consideration, for it reflects his deep appreciation for rule of law, even in the face

---

18. *Paris Newsletter*'s Account, *TMSB*, 353; emphasis added.

of unjust laws. For More, conscientious objection counseled acts of persuasion, not violent reaction—and if those efforts failed, silence remained, it would seem, the only permissible alternative. Because he had not actively opposed Henry or Parliament, More reasonably believed that he should be left alone to die in prison for refusing the oath. Not only that, but this defense tactic had traction under the statute. The Treasons Act criminalized statements as well as conduct that "maliciously" deprived the king of his title of Supreme Head of the Church in England, as conferred by the Act of Supremacy. More argued that "malice" requires some word or deed.[19]

---

19. Scholars disagree whether the word "maliciously" was an element of the offense or surplusage, the mere equivalent of "traitorously," not adding to the definition of the offense. Most recently, H. A. Kelly argued that Parliament added the word "maliciously" in order to raise the burden of proof and, to the extent that the Crown, judges, and jury, disregarded it, More's verdict was unjust. Kelly, "A Procedural Review of Thomas More's Trial," *Thomas More's Trial by Jury* 1. Before Prof. Kelly, John G. Bellamy argued for the former view. Bellamy, *The Tudor Law of Treason* (Toronto: University of Toronto Press, 1979), 32–33.

More found another reason for refusing to answer his interrogators. In the absence of *some* evidence, he maintained, it was impermissible to question him at all and put him in peril of violating the Treasons Act. And what evidence could there be since he was already in prison when the Treasons Act was enacted? While in prison, he recalled that "[n]o one has the power to tender an oath to anyone else binding him to reveal such a secret as can and should be kept hidden. If a general oath is tendered, it is always understood that it applies to misdeeds the knowledge of which was acquired by the swearer in such a way that he can lawfully reveal them."[20] There must be some evidence of a crime in order to place the accused under oath in the first place. The point is summarized by Aquinas in the *Summa Theologiae*: only "when the accused is already disgraced through the commission of some crime, or certain

---

20. *Complete Works*, ed. Guy et al., vol. 6, 765–67.

indications of his guilt have already been discovered, or again when his guilt is already more or less proven," may the accused be placed under oath and forced to answer incriminating questions.[21] More's strategy accords with, and probably has its roots in, an axiom of Western law that commanded wide acceptance "in the English common law and in the European *ius commune*: *De occultis non jurat ecclesia. Nemo tenetur prodere seipsum* [Concerning secret things, the Church does not judge. No one is bound to accuse himself]."[22] In effect, no person ought to be punished for his private thoughts. More plausibly asserted that he had never divulged his opinion of the Act of Supremacy.

Finally, More's silence had a spiritual dimension. It showed his prudence, self-knowledge, and humility. After the passage of the Act of

---

21. Aquinas, *Summa Theologiae* 2–269.2.

22. Richard Helmholz, "Natural Law and the Trial of Thomas More," *Thomas More's Trial by Jury*, 56.

Supremacy, at his first interrogation, More took the position that "I would never meddle in the world again . . . but my whole study should be upon the passion of Christ and mine own passage out of this world."[23] In the last interrogation, he was pressed to "speak even out plain against the statute" if he would rather be out of the world. But self-knowledge dictated a different course: "I have not been a man of such holy living as might be bold to offer myself to death, lest God for my presumption might suffer me to fall, and therefore I put not myself forward, but draw back. Howbeit if God draw me to it himself, then trust I in his great mercy, that he shall not fail to give me grace and strength."[24] More observed in one of his Tower Works, *The Sadness of Christ*, that while there were "those martyrs who freely and eagerly exposed themselves to death," not all of them did so. But More was concerned not "to deny the

---

23. Letter, May 2, 1535, *TMSB*, 345.

24. Ibid., 350.

triumph of those who do not rush forth of their own accord but who nevertheless do not hang back or withdraw once they have been seized, but rather go on in spite of their fearful anxiety and face the terrible prospect out of love for Christ."[25] By not declaring openly his opposition to the king's new title but eluding with legal acumen his pursuers, More avoided the sin of presumption, that is, a misplaced, arrogant reliance on God's power. In the Christian tradition, martyrdom is a grace, a freely given gift. Silence ensured that More did not assume that such a gift was his.

JOY IN SUFFERING

More, in his handling the Royal Supremacy, embodied the virtue of fortitude to a heroic degree. He fully internalized that admonition of Jesus: "Be not afraid of them who kill the body and after that

---

25. Thomas More, *The Sadness of Christ*, trans. Clarence Miller (Princeton: Scepter, 1993), 41.

have no more that they can do."[26] According to the *Catechism of the Catholic Church*, "Fortitude is the moral virtue that ensures firmness in difficulties and constancy in the pursuit of the good. It strengthens the resolve to resist temptations and to overcome obstacles in the moral life. The virtue of fortitude enables one to conquer fear, even fear of death, and to face trials and persecutions. It disposes one even to renounce and sacrifice his life in defense of a just cause."[27]

More conquered the fear of death and sacrificed his life in defense of a just cause. In his writings from prison, he found strength in the example of Christ, above all by meditation on his Passion: "Is it not, then, a stupendous shame for us to forsake our Savior out of dread of temporal death, when he willingly suffered such a painful death rather than forsake us? And especially considering, besides all that, the fact that for our

---

26. Luke 12:4.

27. *Catechism of the Catholic Church*, no. 1808.

suffering he will so lavishly reward us with ever-lasting life."[28] This connection between prayer and fortitude is illustrated in one of the most dramatic passages of *The Sadness of Christ*. More vividly describes the fearful agony of Jesus in the Garden of Olives or Gethsemane—*transfer calicem istum a me* [remove this cup from me]. But through prayer to his Father, Christ emerges with the strength to undergo the rest of his Passion. More draws the lesson that "whoever is utterly crushed by feelings of anxiety and . . . tortured by the fear that he may yield to despair" should "consider this agony of Christ, . . . meditate on it constantly." "For after He had suffered this agony for a long time, His spirits were so restored that He arose, returned to His apostles, and freely went to meet the traitor and the tormentors who were seeking to make Him suffer."[29] More wrote

---

28. *A Dialogue of Comfort against Tribulation* (CTMS ed. 2013), 263.

29. More, *The Sadness of Christ*, 44–45.

that Christ willed to suffer in order, among other things, to "offer this unheard of, this marvelous example of profound anguish as a consolation to those who would be so fearful and alarmed at the thought of torture that they might otherwise interpret their fear as a sign of their downfall and thus yield to despair."[30]

More's courage was so deeply rooted in the virtue of hope—in the conviction that an omniscient and all-loving God is in charge—that it manifested itself in humor. This heroic joy is evident in More's good humor on the scaffold. To the official who escorted him from prison to the scaffold, he said, "I pray you, Master Lieutenant, see me safe up, and for my coming down, let me shift for myself."[31] Hope, the guarantee of heaven, finds its expression in merriment. It is unattainable without fortitude, the habit of overcoming the fears that turn us aside from the goal.

---

30. Ibid., 41.

31. Roper, *TMSB*, 64.

More's hope overflowed in feelings of fellowship toward those who sentenced him to death:

> [L]ike the blessed apostle St. Paul . . . was present and consented to the death of St. Stephen, and kept their clothes that stoned him to death, and yet be they now both twain holy saints in heaven, and shall continue there friends forever, so I verily trust, and shall therefore right heartily pray, that though your lordships have now here in earth been judges to my condemnation, we may yet hereafter in heaven merrily all meet together, to our everlasting salvation.[32]

More's prayer for the salvation of his persecutors is undoubtedly sincere. But by comparing them to St. Paul before his conversion, to Saul who persecuted the first Christians, this parting shot also affirmed the righteousness of his cause and the injustice of theirs.

---

32. Roper, *TMSB*, 61.

CHAPTER 5

More and Heresy

DOES MORE'S TREATMENT OF HERETICS diminish his achievements? Especially for the modern reader, his invocation of conscience and defense of silence raise troubling questions. First, did More commit a moral evil by cooperating in the prosecution of obstinate heretics? Second, was More hypocritical in his silence and in seeking to be left to his conscience when interrogated by the Crown's representatives? In light of More's conduct in prosecuting those accused of heresy, did he deny to others the treatment which he later sought for himself?

More was anything but apologetic about the punishment of heretics.[1] His epitaph, which he drafted after his resignation, includes: "He so conducted himself all through this series of high offices or honors that his Excellent Sovereign found no fault with his service, neither did he make himself odious to the nobles nor unpleasant to the populace, but he was a source of trouble to thieves, murderers, and *heretics*."[2] What was More thinking? He was thinking in the same tradition of nearly all statesmen of his time as to the role of religion in public life; he was thinking about public safety; and, in addition, he was thinking of the good of souls.

The prosecution of heretics by the civil authorities was a fact of sixteenth-century society. Only "obstinate" heretics (that is, public and unrepentant) were prosecuted; in ecclesiastical court

---

1. The total number of heretics burned during More's chancellorship was six. He was actively engaged in the proceedings (as opposed to just signing writs) of three them.

2. Inscription on the Tomb of Thomas More, *TMSB*, 308; emphasis added.

one had to be adjudicated guilty and, then, refuse to abjure before being handed over to the "secular arm" for punishment. To be clear, no one—not on the Catholic side, and not on the emerging Protestant side—held a notion of individual freedom of religion. W. E. Campbell, editor of *English Works of St. Thomas More*, an Anglican writing of the 1920s, states the matter succinctly: "Toleration was in the sixteenth century no more part of the orthodox Protestant creed than it was of Roman Catholicism. Protestants as well as Catholics thought that only one form of truth could be true, and that that form must be preserved at all costs."[3] Uniformity in matters of religion was also believed to be essential to a healthy, peaceful society. Furthermore, it was codified in law and enforced by every European state for hundreds of years before More and for at least another hundred after him. It is anachronistic to judge More

---

3. W. E. Campbell, "The Spirit and Doctrine of the *Dialogue* [*Concerning Heresies*]," in *English Works of St. Thomas More, vol. 2,* (London: 1931), 78.

by a standard that had not even been imagined, let alone formulated, in the sixteenth century.

The prosecution of heretics was supported by at least two rationales: first, *tranquillitas ordinis*, or social peace and order, and, second, concern for the souls of subjects. Religion—particularly, creedal religion—was considered fundamental to the social order. That heresy fomented civil disorder was universally held. As the editor of More's *English Works*, Campbell, explains, "More accepted the stern theory, then held by every civil lawyer in Christendom, that in a Catholic State obstinate heresy should be punishable by death—and that death by burning. For the civil law in those days held heresy to be the worst kind of sedition against the State, since, as was known by experience, it was the most disturbing."[4] This understanding was enshrined in law. England formally introduced the death penalty for obstinate heresy in 1401,

---

4. Ibid.

during the reign of Henry IV, in a measure
entitled *De heretico comburendo* (literally, "concerning the heretic to be burned") in response to
Christian heresies and social upheaval attending the rise of John Wycliffe and Lollardy.[5] As
Chancellor, More was the chief executive and
judicial officer. Contrary to recent portrayals
of More, the prosecution of heresy was not a
private initiative or vendetta; it was, rather, the
law of the land. And the cases were processed
with adherence to established procedures which
favored the accused, at least in comparison to
English criminal procedures.[6] Furthermore, the

5. It was not until March 1677 that Parliament passed a bill
revoking the Crown's right to the writ ordering the execution of an
obstinate heretic.

6. For a discussion of English heresy procedure during More's
lifetime, see Oakley, "English Heresy Procedure in Dialogue
Concerning Heresies," *Center for Thomas More Studies, http://
www.thomasmorestudies.org/tmstudies/DCH_Oakley.pdf*. And for a
study of the inquisitorial procedure, especially as it compares with
extent of civil procedure, see H. A. Kelly, "Inquisitions and Prosecution of Heresy: Misconceptions and Abuses," 58 *Church History*
440 (1989).

connection between heresy and social unrest, not to mention sedition, was real. It was fixed in the English mind by the Peasant's Revolt of 1391, which was bound up with the Lollardy heresy. In More's time, the connection between the Lutheran heresy and revolution was made manifest by the bloody Peasants' War, that great uprising which ravaged central and southern Germany in 1525, causing the deaths of over 70,000 peasants in one summer. More was certain—and correct—that the spread of the Lutheran heresy spelled a social-political upheaval. And the dire consequences of civil unrest, in general, had been seared into English consciousness by the War of the Roses, which did not end until 1487 when the Lancastrian Henry VII secured the throne by marrying the Yorkist Elizabeth. More was not too young to appreciate the horror of civil war. Indeed, the historian of Tudor England, Alistair Fox, no Catholic and no admirer of More writes: "[his] horror of civil violence was as real as his belief in its connection with heresy was genuine.

As early as 1523 he had discerned a potential threat to social and political order on the Continent, and prophesied direly in the *Responsio* [*ad Lutherum*] that heretical subversion of the clergy would lead to anarchy."[7] As Richard Rex, a leading contemporary authority on the English Reformation, puts it in the *Cambridge Companion to Thomas More*, in acting as he did against heresy and heretics in England, "More showed himself to be, not a fanatic, but a statesman."[8]

Rex is on firm ground. In the 1530s in England, the Lutheran heresy was fueled by the party of Anne Boleyn. Not coincidentally, Lutheran theology had gained adherents among the intellectual and commercial elites, as well as at Court, as seen in the ascendancy of Thomas Cromwell in 1531 and the protection afforded

---

7. Fox, *Thomas More: History and Providence* (New Haven: Yale University Press, 1983), 139.

8. Richard Rex, "Thomas More and the Heretics: Statesman or Fanatic?" *The Cambridge Companion to Thomas More*, ed. George M. Logan (New York: Cambridge University Press, 2011), 93.

Luther's English disciple, William Tyndale (for a time). For perhaps principled and certainly pragmatic reasons, Cromwell, that most formidable enemy of More and the English Catholic Church, was an adherent and promoter of Lutheranism. According to Rex, "[More] realized that a new doctrine meant a new order. The facts of his public career suggest that he saw heresy as the greatest political issue facing his times and that he acted on that perception."[9] Thus, certainly during his months as chancellor, the spread of heresy jeopardized England's place in Christendom. The Lutheran challenge to the established order threatened More's most cherished ideal of lasting peace among nations, where monarchs were constrained in their territorial and worldly ambitions by truths of the Catholic faith. In particular, Lutheran ecclesiology—More must have known— would not only rupture the unity of Europe. It would empower kings beyond their considerable

9. Ibid., 111.

prerogatives. Lutheranism was received by the German princes as an invitation to Caesaropapism, modeled after the good kings of Hebrew Bible, such as Josiah, who ruled over the spiritual *and* temporal realms. This political consequence of Lutheran thought must have held an attraction for Henry VIII, especially when the Church in Rome frustrated his marriage plans. In addition to pillow talk, Anne Boleyn probably influenced her husband by supplying him with Tyndale's tracts as well as his (justly famous) English translation of the Bible.

For More, it is important to note, the Lutheran heresy's threat to the *tranquillitas ordinis* went beyond the dismantling of Christendom. As Gerard Wegemer has explained, it threatened public safety itself, as well as, then, the possibility of civic harmony and genuine reform.[10]

Eventually, even Erasmus came out publicly against Luther, having become convinced that his

---

10. Wegemer, *Thomas More on Statesmanship*, 161–182.

teachings would spell the end of unity and peace in Christian Europe.[11]

> As they [More and Erasmus] saw it, reformers like Tyndale and Luther were destroying the traditional supports for law and authority— and, therefore, of peace and unity—by denying free will, by emphasizing the corruption of human reason, and by limiting the Church to an elite group of "pure and spotless" individuals who claimed a nonrational access to the truth of reality. . . . Both . . . predicted that, if the power of reason was denied and if will and private inspiration were to become reason's substitute, the result would be widespread chaos and increased violence.[12]

Violence came, as foreseen, first, in the form of the Peasants' Revolt in Germany in 1523 and the bloody invasion of Rome by Germans in 1525.

---

11. Ibid., 159.
12. Ibid., 13.

Subsequently, the Wars of Religion ravaged Central, Western, and Northern Europe for more than a century.

The other motive for the prosecution of heresy was equally or more pressing to More and religiously minded contemporaries: solicitude for the souls of subjects. They saw damage not only to the secular order but the spiritual. Catholics and Protestants adhered to a severe understanding of the doctrine of *extra ecclesiam, nulla salus* [no salvation outside the Church]. In More's day, the literal meaning was the only meaning. (It was not until 1863 that Pius IX expounded the non-literal interpretation in an Apostolic Letter; and then it was not until 1963, in Vatican II, in *Dignitatis Humanae*, that the Church definitively declared the non-literal meaning to be correct.) Thus, for More, the heretic was worse than a murderer. By leading the faithful out of the Church, he willfully and selfishly destroyed their chances for eternal life. More adhered to the commonly accepted definition of a heretic, to quote from one of his apologetical works, *Debellation of Salem and Byzance*: "all they that obstinately hold any self-minded opinion contrary to the doctrine that the common-known Catholic Church teach[es] and hold[s] for necessary to salvation."[13] "Nothing could be more absurd, in [More's] view, than to go willingly to death on account of a personal opinion. It was precisely this, for him, that characterized the Protestants he condemned. Heresy was the preference of personal opinion over the consensus of the Church, a consensus providentially guaranteed by the Holy Spirit."[14] If the defense of heresy prosecution sounds paternalistic to us, it *should*. The king was considered to be more than a ruler-father figure. For More and contemporaries, a king was *sacral*; he had a divine calling to promote the spiritual as well as temporal

---

13. More, *The Debellation of Salem and Byzance*, 30/4–7, vol. 10, *The Complete Works of St. Thomas More*, also at Center for Thomas More Studies, *http://www.thomasmorestudies.org/docs/Debellation2014-etext.pdf*.

14. Rex, "Thomas More and the Heretics: Statesman or Fanatic?", 97.

welfare of his subjects. As chancellor (and, earlier, as a royal councilor), More was expected to advance the fatherly and sacred mission of the king, as well as the *tranquillitas ordinis*.

In one of the last interrogations in the Tower, Cromwell fixed on the apparent double standard in More's invocation of conscience and silence: as "Chancellor [More] examined heretics and other malefactors. . . . and used to compel them to a make precise answer thereto. And why should not then the King, since it is a law made here that his Grace is Head of the Church, here compel them to make a precise answer thereto."[15] More responded: "there is a difference between those two cases because at that time, as well here as elsewhere through the corps of Christendom, the pope's power was recognized for an undoubted thing."[16] That is, the Church, when speaking authoritatively through

---

15. Letter, June 3, 1535, *TMSB*, 349.
16. Ibid.

a General Council, was infallible. But the law of the realm was fallible. In the case of a conflict with the former, one is not obliged to follow the latter. Conversely, to the extent that the state was aligned with the Church and enforced its teachings, an individual was bound, assuming the state acted in accord with well-established laws. There was no double standard from More's perspective. The state lost its competency to compel consciences in matters of faith once it severed the connection with the Church and acted contrary to her teachings. As More explained in a letter to Margaret, citizens are not morally bound to endorse every civil law merely because it was duly enacted. Such laws may conflict with natural or divine law. "That a law of this kind can happen to be made in any part of Christendom, I suppose no one doubts—the one exception on that point always being a General Council of the whole body of Christendom."[17] More typifies

---

17. Letter from Margaret More to Alice Alington, *TMSB*, 328–29.

pre-Enlightenment man under law. There is no privilege to disobey an infallible law. At the same time, More predicted the Enlightenment solution—although he prayed not to see it—namely, a post-Christendom Europe, a "day that we gladly would wish to be at league . . . with [heretics], to let them have their churches quietly to themselves, so that they would be content to let us have ours to ourselves."[18] This was not yet the world. And for the good of souls and peace of nations, he strove to maintain the unity of Christendom.

Finally, the modern reader might ask whether More, by taking his stand on conscience, sought better treatment than what he dealt out. The answer is no. True, More repeatedly asked to be "left to his conscience" and, repeatedly, with slight variations, said: "Howbeit (as help me God), as touching the whole oath, I never withdrew any man from it, nor never advised any to refuse it,

18. Roper, *TMSB*, 33–34.

nor never put, nor will, any scruple in any man's head, but leave every man to his own conscience. And methinketh in good faith that so were it good reason that every man should leave me to mine."[19] In assessing his consistency, we must note that More rested his claim to be left to his conscience on having maintained silence, on never having expressed any opinion. For, as long as he maintained silence, he had a claim under contemporary legal principles to be left alone, or not to take an oath or to answer questions. The silence of More is the key to seeing that he was consistent in his defense and treatment of heretics. He was not engaged in conscientious objection, not seeking an *exemption* from a general law on account of his conscience. More was certainly not claiming a right to free expression or association. Rather, he asserted that the state did not have the authority to prosecute him, or force him make a statement or to take an oath, concerning a matter about

---

19. Letter, April 17, 1534, *TMSB*, 315.

which he had not shared his view, about which he had kept his own counsel and maintained silence. Rather, silence, arguably—"arguably" because the king, his councilors, Parliament and, ultimately, a jury came to a different conclusion—negated the evidential basis necessary to question him in the first place, let alone to convict him of maliciously depriving the king of his title. According to More, when Chancellor Audley and Master Secretary Cromwell told him "that the King might by his laws compel me to make a plain answer thereto, one way or the other," he responded that, although he "would not dispute the King's authority," his conscience gave him an out.[20] In this way, as explained above, More was invoking a narrow exception to the rule that the accused must incriminate himself. In refusing to answer questions during interrogations in the Tower, he took advantage of the same limitations which constrained—or were supposed to constrain—all

20. Letter, June 3, 1535, *TMSB*, 349.

criminal investigations, including, especially, heresy.[21] In commenting on heresy procedure in his *Dialogue Concerning Heresies*, More was clear that a heresy suspect normally could not refuse to cooperate with an investigation without committing perjury because there simply was no

---

21. The process which regulated the investigation of heresy by the ecclesiastical court was known as *inquisitio ex officio*, from which we derive the (ominous) term, inquisition. As H. A. Kelly demonstrates, the inquisition was "not originally designed as a procedure against heresy or only against heresy." Rather, it was "the universal method of trial procedure in all ecclesiastical courts . . . where plaintiffs brought suits against defendants. . . . For instance, all of Henry VIII's annulment trials were inquisitions." This procedure constituted progress in fairness for the accused. "[It] was devised as a more comprehensive and satisfactory alternative to 'accusation.'" Under the procedure known as accusation or *accusatio*, a private party would accuse someone of a crime and attempt to prove it. Thus, the judge did not take sides but simply decided the contest between two independent parties. In contrast, inquisition required *publica fama*, that is, reputable opinion—evidence—that a certain person is guilty of a given crime. Here one finds the advance in procedural fairness. *Fama* takes the place of the accuser, and the judge himself levels the charge and prosecutes the case. Henry Ansgar Kelly, "Thomas More on Inquisitorial Due Process," *The English Historical Review* CXXIII, 53, August 1, 2008, 123.

right against self-incrimination. Those accused of heresy, as well as those accused of treason, could refuse an oath and/or refuse to answer questions of interrogators only if the examiners exceeded their authority. Royal and ecclesiastical prosecutors could exceed their authority under two sets of circumstances—and both were arguably present in More's prosecution: first, where the tribunal was not authorized by law or was otherwise unjust; and, second, where questions were not based on at least some evidence, or *publica fama*,[22] of something said or done by the suspect.[23] With respect to the requirement of *publica fama*, one who maintained his own counsel, who did not share his views with others, could not be compelled to incriminate himself because,

---

22. The procedural safeguard of *publica fama* was derived from the ancient legal axiom, *"Ecclesia de occultis non iudicat"* ("the Church does not judge secret matters"). Helmholz, "Natural Law and the Trial of Thomas More," *Thomas More's Trial by Jury*, 56–59.

23. More, *Dialogue Concerning Heresies*, 324.

presumably, there was no evidence upon which to initiate an inquiry (lawfully).

In sum, More was ready to leave a man unmolested in his beliefs; however, to share heretical beliefs with one's neighbors or to preach them *in flagrante* authorized prosecution by the ecclesiastical courts and possible punishment by the secular arm. More was not adhering to a double standard because he did not claim a right to free expression or association. The right on which he relied was a constricted one, namely, not to be prosecuted and punished for thoughts, as well as the closely related right to remain silent when conscience demanded. More would not have arrogated to himself the privilege of not answering Cromwell, Audley, and the other royal councilors except that he had not shared his potentially seditious belief with anyone. If he had shared his opinion of the Royal Supremacy, he would not have expected anything except punishment. The civil and ecclesiastical law, More argued, did not reach thoughts. For this reason, he argued, as discussed above, at the conclusion of his trial, but before the case was given to the jury, that the Treasons Act "cannot condemn me to death for such silence" or for following a "conscience [that] does not raise scandal or sedition."[24] More did not insist on a right to silence that he denied to those accused of heresy. They, too, could not be lawfully prosecuted for mere thoughts. Absent reliable evidence that the accused had voiced heretical statements or actively propagated heretical teaching, it was unlawful for a court to administer an oath in order to compel a suspect's admission of wrongdoing. The accused heretic was permitted to maintain silence in the face of such questioning. Thus, More was merely availing himself of the same privilege afforded accused heretics.

---

24. *Paris Newsletter's Account, TMSB,* 353.

CONCLUSION

———— ⌇ ————

RESIGNATION FROM ENGLAND'S highest political office, followed by arrest, imprisonment, forfeiture of a great fortune, and finally execution—what in worldly terms would be the quintessence of failure—were in Thomas More's life the marks of an extraordinary ethical and spiritual victory. To paraphrase St. John Paul, because of "the witness which he bore, even at the price of his life, to the primacy of truth over power," More ought to be "venerated as an imperishable example of moral integrity." Not only did More's witness stand as a monumental achievement on account of the courage which it exacted, but we continue to draw meaning and inspiration on account of the truths for which he suffered and died.

With good reason, Gerard Wegemer entitled his essential biography of More, *A Portrait of Courage*. For the truth of the unity of the Catholic Church, More made incalculable sacrifices—of power, freedom, possessions, family, and, ultimately, life. To take the measure of his achievement, we must remember that he did so practically alone. He was England's "Company," the lone, hold-out juror in More's parable about putting truth before fellowship.[1] Instead of resisting eleven other jurors, More went up against the political, ecclesiastical, and intellectual elite of his day. He held firm to a truth, despite its elusive contours, and without the support of a visible, local community of like-minded men and women. Indeed, his own family, including his beloved daughter Margaret, offered no encouragement and even opposed his decision not to fall in line with the king and Parliament.

---

1. Letter from Margaret Roper to Alice Alington, August 1534, *TMSB*, 326–27.

More knew the perils of untrammeled power. Recall his *History of Richard III*—"these matters be kings' games, as it were stage plays, and for the most part played upon scaffolds"[2] and the *Coronation Ode*—"unlimited power has a tendency to weaken good minds, and that even in the case of very gifted men."[3] Still, the Crown's case against him must have been all the more poignant because it meant the failure of his purposeful engagement with the world, of the "indirect approach" that he undertook to ameliorate governmental errors and excesses. More's advice to Hythloday in Book One of *Utopia*, "you must strive and struggle as best you can to handle everything tactfully—and thus what you cannot turn to good, you may at least make as little bad as possible," proved, at the time, to be as unworkable as his "poor advice" to Cromwell: "in your counsel-giving unto His

---

2. More, *History of Richard III*, 94.

3. More, "Coronation Ode of King Henry VIII."

Grace [the King], ever tell him what he ought to do, but never what he is able to do."[4]

With the Submission of the Clergy, the Oath of Succession, and, then, the Act of Supremacy, More found no room to maneuver politically, although what he wrote, said, and did lives on.

Unable to serve his king in good conscience, he withdrew from public life. When pressed to swear the Oath of Succession and, later, to declare his approval of the king's novel title of Supreme Head, he continued his purposeful engagement with the world, but this time to preserve his life as a private citizen. He refused on the basis of his conscience and maintained silence.

This time, too, the indirect approach failed. Although More had scrupulously avoided any speech, let alone conduct, which could be interpreted as seditious, he was imprisoned for not taking the oath and executed for not affirming the Royal Supremacy.

---

4. Roper, *TMSB*, 43.

More's "failure" is our gain. His imprisonment and execution witness to momentous and ever-timely truths. This is especially true now, with the mounting threats to religious liberty in general and to the Catholic Faith in particular. Nevertheless, one must be careful in recruiting More for the cause of *modern* religious liberty. Our contemporary notion of conscience is keyed to a post-Enlightenment understanding of civil liberty and oriented to the accommodation of a plurality of religious faiths. The modern approach derives from the understanding that religious faith, and the individual's conscientious choices on such matters, cannot or should not be judged in terms of truth. In contrast, for More and nearly all political thinkers of his time, civil authority was to be exercised in accordance with, and on behalf of, the true Faith (whether Protestant or Catholic). More did not strive to vindicate the principle of accommodation for religious dissenters; he advocated traditional legal means for the suppression of heresy. Nevertheless, he stood for limitations on the state's ability to compel the consciences of its citizens. As he explained to Margaret, "no one is bound to swear that every law is well made, or bound under pain of God's displeasure to perform any point of the law that is actually unlawful." No earthly authority may compel one's judgment as to what is good and true, which is precisely what Henry attempted.[5] In keeping with the natural law and the *ius commune* (universal law), More stood for the inviolability of the individual conscience against any community, secular or ecclesiastical. Consistent with the ancient principle, *de occultis non iudicat*, that is, the law may "not judge secret things," the community, on More's view, may only punish conduct, not thoughts and beliefs.

More witnessed to other important limitations on the state: the political community cannot

---

5. For example, in 1539, Henry had Parliament enact the Statute of Six Articles, accurately subtitled, "An Act Abolishing Diversity in Opinions," as it compelled all English citizens to believe in six articles of conservative Christian doctrine.

displace religion; the church ought to be independent. The events of the 1530s in England have rightly been called the Henrician revolution. Notwithstanding the complexities of church-state relations starting with Emperor Constantine in the fourth century, the Act of Supremacy was an unprecedented power grab. More saw it as such, and his principled opposition will forever stand for the independence of the church from the state. Jonathan Swift considered More to be a champion of liberty against tyranny, despite Swift's contempt for More's faith. For Swift, More's courageous opposition to Henry's tyrannical rule made him "a person of the greatest virtue this kingdom ever produced, for not directly owning him to be head of the church."[6]

---

6. Jonathan Swift, "Concerning That Universal Hatred, Which Prevails against the Clergy" (May 24, 1736). In *Gulliver's Travels*, Swift includes More as the sole Englishman among the "*Sextumvirate*" of champions of liberty that included Socrates and Cato the Younger. *Gullivers Travels*, Bk. 3, ch. 7.

More also shows us that the will of the political community is not to be confused with the truth. This point, so prominent in the history of Western Civilization at least as far back as 440 B.C. and Sophocles' *Antigone*, merits special attention today. As shared truths diminish, the power of the state increases. Those who embrace truths no longer commonly held can expect conflicts with the law. And in a conflict between law—with the coercive power of the state behind it—and truth, the truth ought not to yield. More witnessed to the correct personal response in a conflict between the demands of conscience and human law: to resist shrewdly, but never to cooperate in evil at any cost.

We should ever be mindful, however, that More only abandoned politics when he absolutely had to. According the *Paris Newsletter*, his last words were that he "dies the King's good servant *and* God's first." That "and" where one might expect a "but" is a critical aspect of More's achievement. He was loath to withdraw—as he said in *Utopia*, "Don't give up the ship in a storm because you cannot hold back the winds." Participation in public life is an obligation not to be lightly set aside.

More's death remains a powerful admonition to rulers and legislators to respect liberty of conscience. But more fundamentally, it is primarily a compelling reminder to the individual citizen that adherence to the truth, the source of personal integrity, may exact a price. If we are to be guided by More, certainly by his example, and perhaps, for some, by his intercession as well, there is no price too dear.

SUGGESTIONS FOR FURTHER READING

PRIMARY SOURCES

A Thomas More Source Book, G.B. Wegemer & S.W. Smith, eds. (Catholic University of America 2004)

Thomas More, *Four Last Things/The Supplication of Souls/A Dialogue on Conscience* Paperback, ed. Mary Gottschalk (Scepter Pub. 2002)

Thomas More, *The Sadness of Christ* (Yale Univ. Press trans. by Clarence Miller) (Scepter Pub. 1997)

For All Seasons—Selected Letters of Thomas More, ed. Steven Smith (Scepter Pub. 2012)

BIOGRAPHIES

Peter Ackroyd, *The Life of Thomas More* (Nan A. Telese 1998)

John Guy, *A Daughter's Love: Thomas More & His Dearest Meg* (Houghten Mifflin Harcourt 2009)

William Roper, *Life of Sir Thomas More, Knight* (c. 1556), reprinted in *Thomas More Sourcebook*. A student version with notes, edited by G.B. Wegemer & S.W. Smith and published by the Center for Thomas More Studies is available at *http://thomasmorestudies.org/docs/Roper.pdf*

Lives of St. Thomas More (Everyman's Library, 1963), containing Roper's *Life of More* and *The Life of More* by Nicholas Harpsfield (Roper's close friend who wrote during the reign of Queen Mary)

Gerard Wegemer, *Thomas More: A Portrait of Courage* (Scepter Pub. 2012)

STUDIES

The Cambridge Companion to Thomas More, ed. George M. Logan (Cambridge 2011)

Travis Curtright, *The One Thomas More* (Catholic Univ. 2012)

Louis L. Martz, *Thomas More: The Search for the Inner Man* (Yale 1992)

Gerard B. Wegemer, *Thomas More on Statesmanship* (Catholic Univ. 1998)

Thomas More's Trial by Jury: A Procedural and Legal Review with a Collection of Documents, H.A. Kelly, L.W. Karlin, G.B. Wegemer, eds. (Boydell Press 2011) [paperback reissue, 2013]

Thomas More: Why Patron of Statesmen? ed. Travis Curtright (Lexington Books 2015)

For a comprehensive collection of essays, *Moreana Journal* (Edinburgh Univ. Press) *http://www.euppublishing.com/loi/more*